THE WRITINGS OF

WILL ROGERS

V-3

SPONSORED BY

The Will Rogers Memorial Commission
and Oklahoma State University

THE WRITINGS OF WILL ROGERS

"How To Be Funny"
& other writings
of
Will Rogers

STEVEN K. GRAGERT, *Editor*

OKLAHOMA STATE UNIVERSITY PRESS
Stillwater, Oklahoma
1983

Printed in the United States of America
Library of Congress Catalog Card Number 82-80505
International Standard Book Number 0-914956-23-x

CONTENTS

Illustrations courtesy
Will Rogers Memorial
Claremore, Oklahoma

INTRODUCTION

Of the two-million-plus words that Will Rogers put to the printed page during his fifty-five years, the vast majority appeared in one of several uniform series that included the "Daily Telegrams," the "Weekly Articles," the "Letters of a Self-Made Diplomat," and the topically-related material in each of his six books. *"How to Be Funny" and Other Writings of Will Rogers*, which comprises this the twentieth volume in the definitive collection *The Writings of Will Rogers*, a cooperative effort of Oklahoma State University and the Will Rogers Memorial Commission of the State of Oklahoma, diverges significantly from the uniformity of our previous books. Herein appear eighteen articles that Rogers wrote for a varied assortment of magazines between the years 1917 and 1933 and six hitherto unpublished pieces from the collections of the Edmon Low Library at Oklahoma State University.

The first part of this volume, the previously-published writings, varies as widely in subject matter as they do in source of publication. One of the pieces, "How to Be Funny," from whence comes the title of this book, offers an appropriately, and a not-unexpectedly, funny analysis of humor and humorists. Other contributions center on politics, aviation, heroes, show business, chauvinism among states, running, diplomacy, the presidency, prohibition, boosterism, and a myriad assortment of other topics.

While the diversity of the articles is significant, so also is the number of years—sixteen—involved. No other single volume in our collection covers as many years of Will Rogers, the writer, as does this one. Indeed, the first article, "The Extemporaneous Line," which appeared in *The Theatre* in 1917, is the earliest piece of Rogers' work in any of our twenty volumes of his writings.

As important as these first seventeen articles may be, perhaps more significant are the six original manuscripts that comprise the second part of this volume. These later works, which were given in 1972 along with other documents to the Edmon Low Library by Will Rogers, Jr., and in bound form constitute the one-millionth volume for that library, have never previously been published; only a few researchers and other individuals have had the opportunity to see them. Now, for the first time, they are offered for the perusal of the general public.

In editing *"How to Be Funny" and Other Writings of Will Rogers* we have followed closely the format established in earlier volumes in our collection. The texts of the published articles appear as they were given in the periodicals; few original manuscripts were available either to publish or to compare against the magazine copy. In contrast the material in the second part derives entirely from original manuscripts; these are published here with only slight editing as to paragraphing, typographical transpositions, and capitalization. The headings for these latter articles come from those given by Will Rogers at the time they were written. Often the "title" indicated the piece's intended use; for example the phrasing of "For Article on Movies in the Zoos" suggests that Rogers had composed it as a possible "Weekly Article." For both the magazine articles and the unpublished writings we have provided annotations of persons, things, and events that may be unfamiliar to present-day readers. In addition we have provided explanatory notes as to the background of each of the six original articles.

Among the many people and groups that have assisted in the production of this volume, I wish to thank especially Dr. Roscoe Rouse, director of the Edmon Low Library, who has most graciously allowed us to publish the Will Rogers' manuscripts from the library's collections. Dr. Rouse has long been an active supporter of our efforts to publish *The Writings of Will Rogers* and has given generously of his time during the past decade in serving on the advisory board for the project. I thank him and his energetic and highly capable staff.

Heartfelt appreciation also is extended to Dr. Reba Neighbors Collins, director of the Will Rogers Memorial at Claremore, Oklahoma, and Mr. Gregory Malak, curator, for the loan of photographs and documents and for assistance with research and proofreading; Mr. Nick G. Geannopoulos, director of publications for Kiwanis International, for permission to reprint "Quien Sabe Caramba?"; Dr. Lawrence L. Boger, president of Oklahoma State University, and his predecessor, Dr. Robert B. Kamm, for their faithful support; the members of the Will Rogers Advisory Committee at Oklahoma State University, especially the board's past chairman, Dr. George A. Gries, and its present chairman, Dr. W. David Baird, for their reasoned advice and patient understanding; Dr. Smith L. Holt, dean of the College of Arts and Sciences, for his encouragement; and the regents of the university and other members of the administration, faculty, and staff.

Funding for the editorial work of the project has been provided in large part by the State of Oklahoma with the cooperation of the Oklahoma Historical Society. Over the years Mrs. T. S. Loffland, Mr. Sylvan Goldman, the Kerr-McGee Foundation, Phillips Petroleum Corporation, and the late Mr. and Mrs. Robert W. Love have also made worthy contributions to the financial and research needs of the project. To all who have made it possible, we are grateful.

Finally, I close with a particularly warm thank you for the work of Ms. Marina C. Pepper, secretary of the project, and Ms. Judy G. Buchholz, publications specialist for Oklahoma State University Press. Both have continually striven to make this project meaningful and successful, to accomplish our goal of providing in a scholarly, but readable format the complete works of a most remarkable American, Will Rogers. For their supremely talented efforts, I thank them.

Steven K. Gragert,
Editor

PREVIOUSLY
PUBLISHED
ARTICLES

The Extemporaneous Line

The question that every guy asked who used to come to interview me was: "Did you really come from out West?" I got so tired of hearing it that I used to tell them: "No, I'm from New Jersey, but don't you tell anybody." The next question invariably would be: "How did you get on the stage?" Say, anything can get on the stage. Its keeping them off that's hard. A fellow can be the champion soup eater and if he can locate a manager that will set him up behind a bowl, and tell him to go to it—if he can keep the audience amused and the soup holds out—why he's on the stage.

Of late all I am asked is: "Who writes your stuff and where do you get it?" And the surprising answer is: The newspapers write it! All I do is to get all the papers I can carry and then read all that is going on and try to figure out the main things that the audience has just read, and talk on that. I have found out two things. One is that the more up-to-date a subject is the more credit you are given for talking on it, even if you really haven't anything very funny. But if it is an old subject, your gags must be funny to get over.

The first thing is the remark you make must be founded on facts. You can exaggerate and make it ridiculous, but it must have the plain facts in it. Then you will hear the audience say: "Well, that's pretty near right."

Lots of good subjects have been in the papers for days and I can't think of a thing on them. Some of the best things come to me when I am out on the stage. I figure out the few subjects that I will touch on and always have a few gags on each one, but the thing I go out to say may fall flat, and some other gag I just happen to put in out there goes great. For instance, here is an example! "Mr. Edison is perfecting a submarine destroyer.[1] Well they say he only sleeps three or four hours out of the twenty-four. That gives him plenty of time to invent."—That was only a little laugh, but I used it to show the audience that I had read about the invention which had only been announced that day. It happened that at this time New York cafes were closed at one o'clock so I casually added to the remark my sudden thought: "Suppose Mr. Edison lived in New

Theatre Magazine, July 1917

York and Mayor Mitchel made him go to bed at one o'clock; where would our invention come from?"[2] And that was a big laugh.

This illustrates my work. I have to have my idea—all extemporaneous speakers do—but my laugh comes quickly and apparently out of nowhere.

Another thing I read, was that submarines could not operate in the warm Gulf Stream—so I said: "If we can only heat the ocean we will have them licked." That didn't get much of a laugh and I was kinda stuck—but I happened to add, "Of course, that is only a rough idea. I haven't worked it out yet." This last went big and covered up the other.

I was talking of the income tax and how hard it hit our girls in the show, and just happened to mention, "A lot of them have figured out it would be cheaper to lay off."

I start in on a subject and if it is no good then I have to switch quick and lots of times when I come off of the stage I have done an entirely different act from what I intended when I went on. Sometimes an audience is not so good and my stuff that night may not be very good, so it is then you see the old ropes commence to do something. It gets their mind off the bum stuff I am telling and as I often say to the folks in the show, I reach away back in my hip pocket and dig up a sure fine gag, as I always try to save some of my best gags—just like a prohibition State man will his last drink.

In the two and a half years I have been with Mr. Zeigfeld in his Follies and Midnight Frolic where we play to a great many repeaters, I have never done the same act any two nights.[3] I have always changed parts of it and in the Frolics a great many times I have done an entirely new act.

Another thing, I think I do the shortest act of any monologue man and that recommends it. On the Amsterdam Roof I never do over six minutes and in the Follies nine or ten, generally eight.

Picking out and talking about distinguished people in the audience I use quite a little, but never unless I know them personally and know that they will take a joke as it is meant. The late Diamond Jim Brady I always spoke of, as I knew him and he always seemed to take an interest in my little act.[4] Once at a big banquet Mr. Brady recited a little poem which he had written himself. I learned the piece and shortly afterwards one night when he was in the audience I did his poem. This made a great hit with Mr. Brady. My best one on him was: "I always get to go to all the first nights, yes I do. I go with Mr. Brady. He sits in the first row and I stand at the back and if any body cops a diamond I am suposed to rope 'em before they get away with it." He was certainly a wonderfully fine man.

On opening night of the New Midnight Frolic, Lieut. Vernon Castle had just returned from France and was then with Mrs. Castle.[5] Vernon and I had played polo together and he is a regular fellow. I walked over

4

to them, shook hands and said: "Here is one old Tango Bird that has made good," and then I told about how Fred Stone and I got Vernon on a bucking horse once and that was where he got his idea of aviating.[6] I said: "Vernon, we worried about you when you were out there at the front, but not half as much as we worried about Irene in the pictures. Boy you don't know what war is, you should see what your wife has been giving them in 'Patria.' "

All I Know Is What I Read
in the Papers

It's been stated Pres. Harding won't run next time.[1] The Republicans want him to because he is the only man they got that is known.

I think the Democrats are the wisest. They are trying to find somebody to run who ain't known.

See where Prohibition boats have been going out beyond the three-mile limit to seize Booze. Couldn't supply the demand with what they could catch inside the three miles.

They are underselling the Bootleggers now. They got no overhead.

An awful lot of traffic to Europe this year. Well there was a lot in '18 too. But this is a different bunch.

All bringing back souvenirs of the War. And we don't properly support the ones we have.

Everybody from Europe brings back a German Police Dog. I don't see why Germany don't pay their National Debt, they have sold enough dogs to pay it.

I wanted to go over this summer but I figured after I paid my fare I wouldn't have enough left to get a dog. So I couldn't go.

(*Life Magazine*, June 16, 1922)

* * *

Mr. Hughes says the Dardanelles should be kept open.[2] Years ago it is said an American sailing ship come pretty near going through there.

When Congressman Herrick from my home state of Oklahoma heard them arguing over these Dardanelles, he said it was all right to keep them open during the week but that he was for closing them on Sunday.[3]

I see they let Lloyd George out in England.[4] I never saw it fail—when a man starts selling his memoirs he is about through.

(*Life Magazine*, November 23, 1922)

* * *

Clemenceau has been here.[5] It seemed like old times to have someone from Europe with a MESSAGE for us.

I am glad his Propaganda was in regard to the last War and not drumming up trade for a new one.

N. Y. always follows European styles. The Tiger arose at 5 a. m. and had Onion Soup for breakfast. I'll bet that will stop some of these Society Birds from imitating them for a while.

I don't know which would be the hardest. To get a New Yorker up at 5 or to get him to inhale Onion Soup.

Newberry has resigned from the Senate and gone back to his front Porch in Michigan to hiss every Ford that passes.[6]

A Lady was seated in the Senate.[7] I think that is a good idea; it draws people's attention to that body of our Government.

She was only there for a day. That's as long as a Lady could stand it. I wonder how long a Gentleman would last.

(*Life Magazine*, December 14, 1922)

* * *

Will Rogers backstage at the Ziegfeld Follies in Chicago in March of 1922. With Rogers is Mayor John F. Hylan of New York City (with eyeglasses) and Mayor William H. "Bill" Thompson of Chicago (next to Rogers).

See where the Allied Debt Conference in London broke up. Getting harder every day to pay debts unless one of the Parties has some money.

If they could just think of something to use for money.

Germany did, they thought of Marks.

Well, Clemenceau has gone back after telling us what he thought of us. Only bad feature is that it might encourage Lloyd George to come over and give us England's version of us.

Clemenceau is certainly a novelty among Politicians. He says what he thinks and NOT what he thinks he ought to say.

He is the Senator Borah of France.[8]

Hope war don't come, it would strike us at a bad time now. All our men are busy fighting Prohibition either on one side or the other.

It must astonish the ex-Kaiser to realize that he has finally had a successful engagement.[9]

(*Life Magazine*, January 4, 1923)

* * *

Well, Xmas has passed, you can tell by the Neckties. They are getting back to normalcy.

Prohibition Agents threatened to make the old Town dry on Xmas and they did, it was a beautiful day and didn't rain a drop.

Department stores and Bootleggers never had a bigger Xmas, they both had to put on extra clerks and keep open at nights.

The Silver Pocket Flask has supplanted the Xmas Card as our National gift, nothing is more welcome when full, or more bunglesome when empty.

Previously published articles

The New Year opened with many happy returns of the Peace Conferences.

The Husbands being murdered by Wives' Industry kinder dropped off during the Holidays, suppose few Husbands come home.

Wives have figured that it's easier and cheaper to shoot 'em than to Divorce 'em, besides there is no comparison in the publicity.

(*Life Magazine*, January 18, 1923)

Grins and Groans
from the Late Election

You know there is going to be an awful Scandal over this last Election. The Republicans claim the Democrats didn't notify them they were having one.

* * *

That's just like those Democrats, they are kinder dirty that way.

* * *

One Republican in New York City found it out and voted for Miller.[1] And now the Democrats are trying to find out how he knew it. It seems there was a leak somewhere.

* * *

I made one speech for my Man in New York and elected him. While Harding, Hughes and all of them gave the Government's time to help Frelinghuysen in N. J.[2] But the Voters judged him by the Company he had kept.

* * *

Edwards of N. J. just waved a Bottle at the Polls and the Voters come a-running.[3]

* * *

The man with the Bottle is the man of to-day. The only way to beat him is to get two bottles.

* * *

Frelinghuysen had plenty of Bottles but he made the Mistake of opening them for the Cabinet instead of for the voters.

* * *

Life Magazine, December 7, 1922

Senator Calder of New York couldn't survive the Glove Tax.[4] His Pallbearers all wore mittens.

* * *

A Doctor was elected Senator from New York.[5] That means an Apple a day.

* * *

Lodge and Culture had a close call in Massachusetts.[6] The Illiterate element come within five thousand votes of predominating.

* * *

LaFollette of course was elected.[7] A Child born in Wisconsin is taught two things. One is to love LaFollette and the other is to hate Minnesota.

* * *

Hiram Johnson won in Cali-Iowa.[8] You may have seen some slight mention of it in the Hearst Papers.[9]

* * *

And when these all get in there they will be just as bad as the others. Politics is all *Apple Sauce* anyway.

My Rope and Gum
for a Democratic Issue

I have just swung in off a Round-up of the entire United States and Florida. It called for quite a bit of speculation as to just what the trip was made for. Most big concerns send out men to make practical demonstrations of their various commodities and most people thought I was demonstrating So-and-So's Chewing Gum.

You notice I didn't mention any name in there. That's because nobody made it worth while to mention any particular name. They never thought this article would ever get anywhere. I could have put some Firm's name up there where I said So-and-So's just as well as not. Well, all I can say is that they lost a chance of getting their name in a thriving and growing periodical, one which has never had a boom but just a steady and healthy growth. Others thought the Tour was subsidized by Durham, North Carolina, to educate the inhaling and match-scratching population of this great near-Republic on the merits of Durham's Bovine industry. All of which was libelous to me. One—just one, thank Goodness—jealous-natured individual went so far as to suggest that I was jumping around over the country for a filthy financial reason. Nothing could have been farther from the truth than that statement. Why, there was times when I didn't even think about what I was going to get—I had to sleep part of the time.

So as a matter of fact nobody ever knew just why I made that trip, and so that is why I am going to tell it to you now. And the funny part of it, nobody got wise to what I really was out for. It looked like I was just out to tell my little riddles, but all the time I had a mission. I remember one time Mr. Henry Ford said to me when I was at his home in Dearborn and I was talking to him about something some man had just said, and he replied, "Yes, but you never want to judge by talk. Your mouth is just a camouflage of what your mind is thinking."[1] That was a pretty wise crack, and was issued by the smartest man in America.

Henry Ford knows less about books and more about everything else

Saturday Evening Post, May 1, 1926

13

that means something than any man living. Making automobiles is the worst thing he does. So I was like Uncle Henry said—I had kept them camouflaged as to my real object. Now I am not going to be like a lot of our ex-prominent men have been lately—wait until the parties concerned are all dead and then frame up their memoirs and publish them. I will tell you why I went out: I wanted to find a campaign issue for the Democratic Party. So that is the truth of why the tour was made.

Why, you ask, did I want to locate an issue for the Democratic Party? I belong to neither party politically. Both parties have their good and bad times, only they have them at different times. They are each good when they are out, and each bad when they are in. But I did it out of pure sportsmanship, just for the sake of a real race. I have all my life admired great sportsmen such as Thomas Lipton, bless his old Scotch and Soda lined gizzard.[2] He is loved the world over because he is its greatest sportsman. They love him because he loses. It would be a shame to spoil him by having him win. The Keenes, the Whitneys—America is mangy with great sportsmen.[3]

But after all what is the greatest sporting event we have in America? Why, our national election, of course—that is, it used to be. But for the last few years the thing has been deteriorating, and so one-sided that you can't even get an audience to watch it. Some papers have quit publishing the result of them. At the last election they didn't even count the votes, they just used the old tally that was cast for Mr. Harding. Why, in the old days elections used to be so close that people would bet on them. One time, I have heard, it got as close as even money.

Now what has caused this late one-sided or cock-eyed situation to arise? Why, an issue, of course; so that is why I took it upon myself to go out and see if I couldn't dig one up. You ask, what would have been my reward? Why, the reward of a true sportsman, the reward of seeing a real race. If I could have found an issue I would have gone down in the sporting annals of American History—that would have been my reward. If I could have found an issue, think what we could have witnessed at the next election! Why, it would have been published in the papers what day the election was to be held on. People would have held meetings again. I wouldn't be surprised if they would have buttons with pictures on them again. New York would get back to its old habit of voting at just as many precincts as you would haul them to.

Wanted Opponents, Not Victims

Why, the last few elections people haven't even taken interest enough to vote once, much less all day. Just think if I had been responsible for creating an election where people would have fist fights at the polls like they used to. If I could have unearthed an issue, think what would have

14

happened even in the White House. Instead of Mr. Coolidge pressing an electric button opening the Prune Preservers Political Powwow at Fresno, California, he would have been there opening it personally, and telling them what he would do if reelected for that great wrinkled industry, and how he had never eaten a grapefruit for breakfast in his life.[4] Instead of reading his speech over the radio and saying good night, he would be out there on the platform saying good night personally, while wiping perspiration with one hand, shaking the hand of a colored voter with the other and kissing a female district leader's baby, all simultaneously and at once.

Those are some of the things that would have happened if I had been successful in my research work. Why, a Democratic issue would have replaced High School drinking parties as a national topic of conversation. I don't say the issue would have won; it don't matter if it wouldn't, but it would have made a race. That's what we want again—a race. We don't want to be compelled just to bet on the size of the majority; we want to bet on which one will win.

I could fight Jack Dempsey and you could bet on it.[5] Of course, you wouldn't bet on who would win, but you would bet on how many feet out of the ring he would knock me, or how long it would take me to come to. I wanted to get politics back on a competitive basis.

There is no use in the Democrats meeting every four years and just drafting a victim. What they want to start doing again is to nominate an Opponent. In some competitive events it is still an honor, and you are also the recipient of considerable cash, to finish second in a race, but politics is not listed among these games. They have never been able to dope out second money in a political race. I wanted to bring elections back where they occupied almost as much importance as the World's Series or the Champion Horseshoe Pitching Contest.

I figured it out and I said it can't be the candidates themselves. Here was Jimmy Cox, a fine man, and Governor of a great state.[6] He never stopped a strike, I'll admit, but on the other hand, he never allowed one to get started. He had never been in the Senate, but that should have been an asset instead of a liability. The Senate has furnished more officeholders and less Presidents than any industry we have. He and his opponent were both from the same state and both were newspapermen. Yet he was beaten so far that we thought he got the directions of the course mixed up and had started the other way. Yet I doubt if there was a single vote cast against him for personal reasons. Then four years later they had what they humorously called another election. What happened that time? Why, they stayed in convention so long trying to pick out a man that the election was over before they could get a picture made of him to show the voters who he was.[7] The money they should have spent in the campaign they spent on convention hotel expenses. When they finally adjourned through exhaustion their treasury was as flat as the back of a bob-haired girl's head.

Yet if ability or previous condition of servitude amounted to anything, which of course it don't, why, the man they picked had everything. He had held some of the highest and most responsible positions in the gift of our country. He had been our ambassador to England—and we always kid England and make them think they are the most important of all our foreign embassies. He was one American that could converse with an Englishman without the aid of an interpreter. He had been elected head of the American Bar Association—that's a gang of Lawyers who think that if you are not one of them you are in rompers intellectually. He was good enough to be at their head—and they take that association as serious as a Chamber of Commerce does a cold-potato luncheon.

A Tight Rope for a Platform

We breed race horses for class and they generally run true to form, but not so in politics. John W. Davis had class to burn.[8] Some claimed he had worked for Morgan & Company. My Lord, that's all we all do—work for Morgan, only he was smart enough to get paid for it—and we pay Morgan.[9] Well, what happened? Why, they gave him a platform to run on called Honesty. The voters got to laughing at it so much they couldn't go to the polls. It wasn't a platform; it was a tight wire. Bird Millman from the Ringling show couldn't have stayed on it with two umbrellas.[10]

Honesty in Politics! If the Democrats could have brought back to life Thomas Jefferson, he couldn't have carried his own precinct on that platform. Of course, Mr. Davis was defeated. Another good man bit the dust for the lack of a ground plan. No higher type of man personally ever signed an entry blank, but you can't run on nothing.

The Democrats have got to have some motive besides the salary. So I just wanted to try to keep another good man from being ashamed to stay up and listen to the returns in 1928. I hit out through the North first, New York State, but they were so busy with their smuggling from Canada that I couldn't find out anything from them. They have but one ambition, and that is to show New York City that they are not the whole thing. That's their life issue.

I even went so far as to have a Thanksgiving dinner with Norman Mack at his home in Buffalo, thinking maybe he had heard something, for I knew he had been running with his nose to the ground for eight years, trying to pick up an issue scent.[11]

I didn't let him know my business; I just let on I was there to see Niagara Falls, as when I was married I didn't have enough money to go there. I just casually asked him about an issue; you know, as though there was no importance to it—kind of like a Chicago crook shooting only one man.

Mr. Mack replied, "I can't even pick up a back track to bark at."

I could just tell the way he said it that he would give his whole printing press for an issue. So all I got from him was a meal, which had no political nourishment whatever. I thought to myself, the best way to find out your opponent is to go among his own people and see if you can't kick over an old skeleton somewhere. So I went over into New England. I had seen pictures of the old New Englander with the straw in his mouth who was supposed to know everything. But he had left the farm and moved to town, and when they do that it just lessens their real political knowledge about 70 per cent. A man in the country does his own thinking, but you get him into town and he soon will be thinking second-handed.

I tried to smoke 'em out about Calvin, but "they reckoned as how Calvin was about as economical as you could get 'em, and that was about the only issue there is in Politics."

And come to think about it they were pretty near right. I kicked myself because the Democrats hadn't thought of this economy stuff first. They had been running on it for years, but it was under the title of Lower Taxes. But people had got so used to it and it had never been carried out that they didn't take it as a platform any more. But they had never thought of changing it and calling it economy. You know a title means an awful lot nowadays.

I even went so far as to go into Boston. But I wasn't smart enough to understand anything there. Everything was over my head. All I could hear was Mayflower and traditions. I talked to the Editor of the Boston Globe. I saw he had been snooping same as me, but he hadn't had any luck. I wanted to get in to talk to the Transcript because I had never heard of them being in doubt about anything.

But the office boy said, "What year?"

I said, "What year? What do you mean—what year?"

He replied, "Why, what year did you come out of Harvard?"

I had to tell him that I had never even come *by* Harvard; that I was so ignorant that I had never quite finished Yale. I tried to tell him that I was Roger Williams and had reversed my name to protect it when I went on the Lecture platform.

No Help From Indiana

Well, I soon realized I didn't speak good enough English to understand anything around there, so I lit a shuck for the Middle West, to Indiana, where bad Grammar and worse roads stopped me. I thought to myself, if there is a place in the world where a man ought to get a political tip, it's in Indiana. Children in Indiana are born in voting booths and are weaned on ballots. I hunted up my old friend Will Hays.[12] He happened to be at his home. He had just received his week's pay. He was sitting in his old cabinet chair counting thousand-dollar bills and reviewing Hollywood's latest children's matinée production called More Naked Than Sinned Against.

I asked him, "Bill, what chance do you think the Democrats have in the next Presidential election."

He started laughing and made a note on the back of a fifty-thousand-dollar certified Adolph Zucker draft, and then replied, "Thanks, Will; I was just making a note of that remark of yours. I will wire it out to the coast. It'll make a great title for a comedy."[13]

I then asked diplomatically, "What do you think will be their issue?"

He threw away a torn bill and replied, "Why, are they going to have one this time?" He then beckoned to one of his twelve secretaries—you see, the picture had been running all this time—and said to her, "Look up our record and see if that man playing the villain didn't vote Democratic at the last election, and if so wire the Studio that he is not the right type for the future. We have to keep these pictures clean; they are showing them in churches now."

I then hunted up Mayor Lew Shank, of Indianapolis.[14] He was standing backstage just ready to go on for his vaudeville turn. I said, "Lew, what will be the Democratic issue in '28?"

He said, "Excuse me, I have to go on. That Dog act has just finished; ask them." Had that wonderful man of Indiana, Tom Marshall, been living, my search might have ended.[15] He had humor and horse sense.

I then tried Tom Taggart.[16] I knew every man or woman over voting age in the state of Indiana can't order an extra helping of pie without having it sliced by the Taggart machine.

I asked him, "What do you figure will be the issue of the Democrats?"

He acted about half sore, and said, "Who sent you to ask me that fool question?"

The Nucleus of an Issue

Then I stepped across the line over into Illinois and tried Mr. Lowden.[17] He had always appealed to me as being a smart man, as I had seen him refuse the Vice Presidency. He has always been more or less interested in the farmer, and has watched them through all their foreclosures.

I said to him, "Mr. Lowden, I know it's not your party, but what can the Democrats possibly use as an alibi for a race in '28?"

He said, "Well, it did look like Relief for the Farmer was their one best bet for a few minutes, but Coolidge guessed it as quick as they did and he rushed out to Chicago and spoke to the farmers, not over the radio, but personally. Serious cases require serious remedies. He told them he knew they were not satisfied with conditions, but neither was he. Well, that seemed to soothe them back to their mortgages."

Just to be uneasy and to know that the President is uneasy with you is a mighty big help, so the Democrats lost that chance of an issue.

Well, I got out of Chicago as quick as I could, because I didn't have on any steel jacket. I got into Michigan and struck Jim Couzens.[18]

I asked, "Mr. Couzens, what could those Democrats possibly make an issue out of?"

"Why, Mellon, of course! That's the only issue in this country—is Mellon going to ruin us or not? Mellon is the biggest issue since slavery."[19]

"But, Mr. Couzens, the Democrats have already voted to uphold his Tax Bill. They not only saw his $250,000,000 cut which he advised, but they raised him $135,000,000."

He replied, "Well, I don't care if they did; he's my issue, anyway, even if the Democrats don't want to use him as theirs."

Well, I then hurried across Pennsylvania as fast as I could, for any state that is too hot for General Butler to stay in is certainly no place for a nervous person.[20] I run into Maryland so fast I went clear through it before I could stop. I hunted up my old friend Governor Ritchie.[21] He sure didn't hesitate—he gave me an issue right off the reel: "Repeal of the Volstead Amendment and the right of every state, even down to Rhode Island, to pick out its own rules without the interference of the Federal Government."[22]

Well, come to think of it, he did have the nucleus of an issue at that. If I hadn't known that politicians are not all like Ritchie, and vote as they think, I would have thought that I had found the issue. So I moved on to Washington. There is really only one person in Washington you want to go to if you want political information. And I felt fortunate in having that one as my friend.

I said, "Alice, what do you think is the footing that the Democrats will probably use in the forthcoming Presidential Handicap?"[23]

She replied, "Will, they are in the mud, as far as the campaign tracks are concerned now. If they went to the Post tomorrow on a hardwood floor, they would be running on soapsuds."

"Well, that's what I have been getting from everybody, but do you think Nick would know some possible issue?"[24]

"Now if I don't, he wouldn't," came the apt retort.

"But, Miss Alice, the Presidential election is two years off. Is there any chance of anything showing up in the meantime?" I asked.

She says, "That's our business—to see that nothing shows up. We are setting in there playing a defensive game from now till November, '28. I won't even allow Nick to change his tie for fear he will make a mistake and the color scheme will offend someone. Even Mr. Coolidge is coached so he won't commit himself to say either yes or no. His reply is, 'I will take it under advisement.' You know, Will, Nick has most of the Democrats with him as it is now. Half of them in the House have forgotten who elected them. If he can just win over about half a dozen cuckoo Republican Congressmen who still believe the common people will rule, why, then he can have it so all Congressmen could go back home and Nick could just phone up their votes from here every day."

"Well, thank you, Miss Alice. Now would you mind telling me this: In case Mr. Coolidge should decide he don't want to hold this office for life, and that he would like to get out and get in something with some excitement to it, do you think Nick would be the boy to step in there? You know that's what they all say—that he has ambition to have the secret-service men guarding him."

"Well, I can't tell you what he will do. I haven't made up his mind yet. Paulina is hardly old enough yet to enjoy the social advantages of the White House that she would a few years later.[25] Nick is young and we are just building now."

Dawes' Tip to the Democrats

Well, I tickled Paulina under the chin and remarked how much like her Grandfather—on her mother's side—she looked. And just as I was taking my leave, why, I found that Senator Borah was next in the conference line.

I said, "Hello, senator! How is the world?"

"Rotten," he replied, without even rising to a point of order.

"Well, senator, some of it must be all right. You have no cause to complain; you Republicans are being paid twice a month. What is the matter with the Republicans, anyhow?"

"Rotten," he snapped at me.

"And the Democrats—what about them?"

"Better than the Republicans, but there is still room for a whole lot of improvement."

"How is Idaho, senator?"

"Terrible! I haven't been there in years."

"Senator, what do you think will be the issue the Democrats will make in 1928?"

"They lost the only one they ever had—that was the World Court.[26] American voters have refused twice, by some 8,000,000 majority both times, to be entertained in Europe's Living Room. Then when the Republicans offered to set them out in the kitchen, the Democrats fell for it and joined. They stepped right out from under an issue there. They

20

have joined the Republicans so much now that they can't blame them for anything that has been passed."

"Then you don't think much of the World Court, senator?"

"Think much of it? Why, half those nations are fighting now, and the rest will be in before a policeman can arrive."

I struck on down the street and run into Dawes, who had two plans, one European and the other American.[27] The European one worked. I knew he was a man who had done a lot of listening lately and might know how the wind was blowing, because I knew he had heard enough of it blow in that Senate.

"Mr. Dawes, what will be the Democratic issue when they start to run next time?"

"Issue! Run! Hell an' Mariar, are they going to run again?"

"Why, yes, I guess so, Mr. Dawes. I think they have to in order to keep up their franchise. Couldn't you suggest an issue?"

"Hell an' Mariar, yes, I could suggest a ____ good issue. Stop unlimited debate in the Senate—that's the biggest issue before this country today. Hell an' Mariar, there's their issue right there. Me, I will join 'em on it too. Hell an' Mariar, yes!"

Issues, Issues Everywhere

"But, Mr. Dawes, you forget. Do you think you could ever get a politician ever to agree to stop talking? That's all they are getting out of politics nowadays. It's kind of tough to deny them that. You might get a nonsalary bill put through, but you will never get a short-talk one passed. They'll sacrifice pay, but they won't sacrifice words. In your reform of the Senate, Mr. Dawes, you are embarked on one of the surest-fire lost causes I have ever heard of. Perpetual motion is a pipe compared to your life's task."

I walked on out of the Willard Hotel—I listened and I heard a noise. I said, "What's that?"

And the door man at the hotel said, "That's Coley Blease telling the Senate something sensible, but they don't want to listen to it."[28]

So I hopped right in a taxi and started for the Capitol. I had the same fellow driving me that drove Dawes the day he slept a man out of the cabinet.[29] I got a hold of Mr. Blease just as he was finishing and asked, "Mr. Blease, I have been all over your state of South Carolina in search of a Democratic issue. Been to Greenville and viewed Bob Quillen's statue to Eve, the mother of all issues.[30] Searched for an issue or a hotel in Rock Hill. So please give me something to base our 1928 Derby on."

"Issue! Issue!" he whispered boisterously. "We got the biggest issue in the world. Are the foreign embassies in Washington going to be allowed to have all the good likker they want right under our noses at European

21

prices, and us have to pay bootlegger prices for poorer stuff? No, sir, I claim that an ambassador ain't much better than a Senator; in fact some of 'em ain't as good. If anybody is going to get cheap likker here, I want to see the Senate get some of it. These embassies are ruining our wimmenfolks' tastes with this good likker. Either make these ambassadors drink the same kind we have to drink or don't let 'em have any. It's the class of likker I'm a-kicking on, not the amount. There's your issue right there." Funny part about the whole thing is that Coley was about right, at that.

Who do I run right smack dab into after I left the Pullman section of the Capitol, and started down to the day-coach end, but my old friend Congressman Upshaw, of Georgia, suh.[31] He was just emerging from that hive of iniquity.

"Mr. Upshaw, I can't find a board for the Democrats to make a platform out of. At the present time they are on a slick log. What do you think will be their ultimate underpinning?"

"Why, we got but one issue; it's the only issue before the country today. It's not only a plank, it's our Gibraltar. We must beat the booze-soaked Republicans and come out flat-footed and pigeon-toed on Prohibition. That's the biggest issue since Remember the Maine."

"But, Mr. Upshaw, we already have that. We can't make something out of something we already have."

"Well, I'm in favor of making it stronger. I want another amendment to read as follows: 'If anybody is caught thinking about drinking, it's a misdemeanor.' And if we can't keep 'em sober on this half of one per cent law, why, let's cut the percentage down. I am for making the amendment read 'An eighth of a quarter of one per cent.' We can beat 'em on that. Show them that America is still composed of decent people. Yes, sir, Prohibition is not only our issue but will always be our issue."

Well, we certainly all appreciate Mr. Upshaw's sincerity in this matter, and the funny thing about it is that he has got it about right, at that. It was a week day and Nick had an understudy presiding over the House, so I thought if it ain't important enough for him to be there, I don't see why I should worry about going in. So I drifted back up to the first class. Nothing was doing even there. I was getting desperate by then, when somebody advised me to go to Florida, because they said if you have lost anything or anybody and you don't know where they are, they are in Florida. So I went down there. My train was right on time to the minute, twenty-four hours late into Jacksonville. Then we started South. We pulled out a little ways and the train stopped apparently for no reason at all. I asked a brakeman what the delay was. He said we were waiting for the conductor.

"Where is the conductor?"

"He took a party out to see a subdivision he is interested in. They will be back in a little while if they don't have trouble with the boat."

While we were waiting the engineer passed literature through the train advertising Headlight Shores and Throttle Terraces. It insinuated in the folders that these were really backed by Averell Harriman, Louis Hill and Helen Gould Shepard.[32] It read like a real double-track development. The fireman seemed sort of out of place among all this activity. All he had to offer was some resales on Coral Stables. The news butch was selling blue prints. I asked him for a morning paper.

"Where you from, mister, Oklahoma? Say, I ain't sold a newspaper since Carl Fisher manufactured his first island.[33] But here is a map of Parcel 23 that we are opening Thursday at 3:15 p.m. at Boco Raccoon. It will be all gone by 3:23. We stop the train and show it to you. Put on your old clothes and go along. Better get in, mister. Henry Ford, Al Smith, Peggy Joyce, Ben Turpin, John Roach Straton, Vincent Astor and Tiger Flowers have all just started building."[34]

No Democrats Allowed

Finally we got started, and met five other trains on the switch trying to get out of there. Our baggageman yelled out to a mail clerk on a train coming from Miami, "What kind of a trip, Bill?"

"Rotten, Jim. The cheap skates are coming in now; got rid of only four binders."

Well, I commenced to get disgusted. I didn't want a lot; I was there on a mission. I wanted to know if there was a possible chance of getting a Democratic issue out of Florida. We reached Miami that same month. I went to Mayor Ed Romph.[35] I had heard he was a live Bird, and I asked him, "Ed, are the Democrats doing anything down here about an issue?"

"Democrats? Democrats? I haven't heard of that company around here. Maybe they are operating over on the West Coast. There is an awful lot of cheap developing going on over there. If they are catering to old people, it's over there."

I just shook my head and left him holding his maps.

I then made for Carl Fisher at Miami Beach. I knew he was the man that had robbed the barracuda of its home and replaced it with apartment hotels.

"Mr. Fisher, you are a smart man. You knew when to leave Indiana. Can you tell me just how the Democrats stand down here, and what chances they have for the future?"

"Well, we won't sell to them over here at all. We got to be awful careful here. We have to protect our original purchasers. No, they haven't got much chance around here. Some places may let the Democrats in, but we are not bothered with 'em much here."

Well, I got disgusted; but as I was leaving the state, I thought I would stop at Tallahassee and see Governor Martin.[36] He ought to know something. I got there just in time. He was just selling the last lot on the Capitol grounds. Some New Yorker had already bought the Senate Chamber for a Night Club.

A Faulty Approach

When he got his commissions straightened out I asked him, "Governor, I have come from California and I can't find anything out there in the way of a Democratic Issue. I thought I would come to you."

"California! California! G-r-r-r-r-r!" And he seemed to go mad and started chewing a corner stone that had been put there to commemorate the spot where Ponce De Leon had searched for the Fountain of Youth, and then went away and died a young man. "California! Our Grapefruit is ten times as sweet as theirs. California! Bah! Bah! They make me sick."

A Seminole Indian who had starved there all his life led me away and apologized for the Governor's conduct. He said I just happened to approach the Governor wrong; that if I hadn't mentioned California perhaps the Governor would have answered me civilly, even affectionately, and perhaps sold me the Governor's office in the Capitol.

Well, this seemed like such a nice fellow, this Indian, and such a Gentleman, that I asked him how is it that he was not selling lots in Florida, being a native and knowing the country and its possibilities. He should be a Star salesman.

He said, "I am an Indian—I have a conscience."

I left that state and hit for Alabama. They told me there was no use stopping in Georgia, as I had just left Georgia in Florida. There is nobody left in Atlanta but a watchman, who forwards the mail. I hunted up our old friend Bill Brandon, Governor of Alabama, at Montgomery.[37]

I asked him, "William, what is the probable issue?"

He threw back his shoulders and threw his chest out and broadcast the following: "Alabama Votes 24 Votes for Oscar W. Underwood."[38]

I grabbed the first train for Mississippi and stumbled over Pat Harrison, who was home on a lot-selling expedition at Gulfport.[39]

Pat is getting so rich he will be able to move over to the Republican side of the Senate within another year.

"Pat, you had the Keynote speech last year. What is it going to be next time? What's the big growl against the Republicans?"

He answered, "Issue? There ain't but one issue. Coolidge is playing Politics—that's what he is doing. He is just using his office for political purposes. That's the issue—make our President stop playing politics. I told it to 'em too."

I thought that is a very truthful issue. Pat is right about it, but the hard

24

part would be convincing the people that Mr. Coolidge had a monopoly on playing politics.

Well, I was getting desperate by this time, so I took a last chance and headed for Austin, Texas. I knocked at the Mansion door and asked, "Is the Governor in?"

"They are," replied the Maid as I went in and met all of them. It seemed that the Governorship was a kind of a family affair. They have two more terms to go, as they have two daughters.

I asked Mrs. Ferguson, "Can you tell me what the Democrats have agreed on as an issue in Texas for the forthcoming Republican festivities?"[40]

"The Democrats never agreed on anything in Texas. That's why they are Democrats; if they could agree with each other they would be Republicans. If Woodrow Wilson was brought back to life and was running for nomination, he would be opposed by twelve different factions.[41] Haven't they in the past year in Congress joined the Republicans rather than belong to each other?"

"I think you have some basis for your logic, Governor—or—er—I mean Mrs. Ferguson."

"I would like to say a word, if you don't mind, Mr. Rogers," spoke up Mr. Jim Ferguson.[42]

"By what right do you want to spiel, Mr. Ferguson?" I asked.

"By right of Governor. I am the only Governor in the world by marriage. The issue is Dan Moody.[43] Dan Moody says I paid too much for concrete and he says I turned out too many prisoners. Dan Moody wants my office—er—er—rather, he wants my wife's office. I didn't pay no more for concrete than they asked. I didn't let out anybody only those that wanted to be let out. Dan Moody don't recognize a man with a heart. That's the issue, I tell you—it's Dan Moody."

Jim Reed, American

"I certainly appreciate your humanitarian feelings, Jim, for everybody likes to see a man with a heart. But do you think putting a heart into Dan would be of enough national importance to elect a President on? You know, if we start putting hearts in people we are liable to be delayed on our road to the White House so long it will be a monarchy before we reach it."

I had to get back by this time, as my funds were running low. I had covered a lot of ground and hadn't seemed to get anywhere. I hated to ask Baruch for any more money.[44] He had done so much for the cause already. Still, I knew how he did want an issue. But I started in, and on the train east from Kansas City, who should be on but Jim Reed.[45] Well, I thought, an Angel sent from heaven. Jim Reed, the very man I should have gone to in the first place.

I buttonholed him, saying, "Mr. Reed, you being one of the most prominent of Democrats and a leader in your party, can you give me an inkling of what the coming fuss will be over, and what if any will be the reason for an election?"

"Who's a Democrat? By what right do you come here to insult me? I am no leader. If I was their leader, they would be going a different way. Moses couldn't lead that gang."

"Well, then, Mr. Reed, perhaps you are a Republican."

"No, I am not a Republican, I am an American, I mind my own business. I am not a Sheep herder for the rest of the world. If they want to shear each other over there, it's none of my business. If they want to have a Kangaroo Court over there, let them have it. If they can't run it on the level without me they wouldn't run it on the level with me. I lived to be able to say, 'I told you so twice.' Mind our own business is our issue, but they won't use that. They will pick out: 'Is aluminum a Trust or is it a Mellon,' or 'Why should it cost so much to run the Mayflower?'[46] That's about the issues they will wind up on."

A Man Who Never Slips

I left him chewing up a New York Times Editorial entitled Benefit to Humanity. I reported back to Barney in New York. My last expense-account nickel had been spent to furnish a platform for other people to stand on in the Subway. He got one look at my face and knew that I had failed. There were tears in his eyes as I related to him what I have told you. He could hardly speak.

"I would willingly pay for another election, Will, if they would just give me a real race, if we could just make it close. Oh, what will the War Industries Board think of me at their next dinner? I don't mind paying for them all the time if I could just announce one ray of hope. And poor Jimmy, this will kill him; he did want to go back to Germany so bad."[47]

"Jimmy? Jimmy who?" I asked.

"Why, Jimmy Gerard. Does anybody hold out any prospect of an issue? Surely the man can't be perfect forever, and to think he might have been born in the South instead of Vermont, and been one of us. But I suppose we wouldn't have recognized him."

"Well, I am as sorry as you are, Mr. Baruch; I am a sportsman at heart. But still there are other losers worse off than us. Think of Harvard. We can do nothing but wait, watch and pray. We can't have too many strings out. Remember, Roosevelt made a colossal political blunder at the last minute and lost a house rent free for four years.[48] Now this fellow can't be so much smarter than he."

"Oh, but that's all I have heard for years is, 'Wait, his foot will slip,' but it don't slip. His feet seem to be inspired. He must wear spikes even when barefoot. Can't you think of something? Where is your head, Will? I am so desperate I will go to anybody for ideas, even you. What can we do? What can we do?"

"Well, Mr. Baruch, the only thing I see is to join them."

Florida Versus California

A Debate Held Before the Prevaricators' Club of America
BETWEEN: Florida in This Corner and California in This Corner.
Both Members of the Club. California is a Charter Member.

FLORIDA OPENING: Ponce de Leon discovered Florida in his search for the Fountain of Youth.

CALIFORNIA REPLYING: Yes, and the Ponce left there and died at an early age. We won't say that his sojourn in Florida shortened his life, but he died soon after, and circumstantial evidence is accepted in many courts. It has been recorded that regret killed him—regret that he couldn't live to reach California. We will admit that the Ponce left quite a reputation, but it was not for discovering Florida; it was for the being the father of the gland seekers.

FLA.: When the United States first bought Florida, they gave only five cents an acre for the land. Ten years ago a dollar an acre would have bought half the state, while now land which is under water is being sold for farming land at $300 and $400 an acre.

CAL.: Yes, Spain sold it for five cents an acre and Spain was never noted for her generosity. The whole history of Spain proves that they always got everything a thing was worth. Yes, and where did the United States get the nickel an acre to pay Spain? They had to stand 'em off till finally they struck gold in California, when one miner, after working all day in the mother lode, returned to his cabin, wearily removed his shoes and just casually shook out enough gold dust to pay for the Florida purchase. That was without even shaking his socks out at all. Now about that land under water selling at $300—we don't know anything about that. We haven't disposed of all ours on top yet, but I doubt if it would be a profitable enterprise out our way. The difference in the intelligence of the buyers might act against us on sales like that; but as your people buy more under water they will naturally get wiser, and in time to come your subterranean farms will decrease.

FLA.: This does not, however, explain the tremendous rush to our

---

Saturday Evening Post, May 29, 1926

shores; Florida passed a law whereby state income tax was free here.

CAL.: We in California make no appeal to tax dodgers. If a man is not patriotic enough to help maintain the state in which he resides, we don't want him in California. Generosity with state as well as with our fellow man is one of our characteristics.

FLA.: Florida is the second largest state east of the Mississippi.

CAL.: Say, what do we care about east of the Mississippi? We are like Al Smith when the Democratic delegation asked him at the continuous Democratic roll call at Madison Square Garden during '24, '25, and '26, "What states do you think you can carry in the South?" Al kiddingly answered them, "Lord, I don't know what states you got down there." So what do we care for east of the Mississippi? Why don't you come out west of the Mississippi, where states are states and men marry governors?

FLA.: Florida is nearly as large as New England.

CAL.: Nearly as large as New England? That old "nearly" ain't going to get you anywhere. Firpo was nearly as good as Dempsey.[1] Now you can't find him. Why, the city of Los Angeles, at every election, annexes more territory than Georgia and Cuba combined. If that state line hadn't stopped us we would have had Phoenix, Arizona. But what's the size of a state got to do with how good it is? I heard of one fellow that was satisfied with Rhode Island, and part of his garage lopped over into Connecticut and half his yard was in Massachusetts. Now if Florida gets to monkeying with us, we will drop 'em down in the middle of the Mohave Desert.

FLA.: We have the longest seacoast of any state in the Union. We have 1145 miles, and that is 100 miles more than California has.

CAL.: Now you notice they emphasize the word "California." Why didn't they say how much more they had than New York or West Virginia. No, they must outdo California. Now what has a long seacoast to do with the quality of a state? According to the latest returns from Rand McNally, Siberia has quite a mess of seacoast, but I have never heard of any emigration going there—that is, voluntarily—on account of their seacoast. Clam diggers and lighthouse keepers are the only two professions that I know of that thrive off long coast lines.

FLA.: We have 3,000,000 acres of Everglades, and when they are drained they will support 3,000,000 people.

CAL.: California has 20,000,000 acres of mountains, and when they are leveled out they will support the whole of India, with the Chinese nation invited as week-end guests. I know you may ask, "Who is going to flatten the mountains?" Why, the same fellow that drains the Everglades. In fact, to show them that there is no hard feeling, and that we don't even look on them as a competitor, we will give them enough dirt to fill up their Everglades. They can't drain their Everglades, as there is nowhere to put the water. If they drain them into the ocean, why, that will raise the ocean higher than the land.

FLA.: Lake Okeechobee has 1,000,000 acres in it. If drained, it would support 1,000,000 people. In one year it produced $1,000,000 worth of catfish.

CAL.: Why, even the name "Okeechobee"—you can't say it without sneezing, and if you speak it enough you are subject to asthma. They say 1,000,000 acres and $1,000,000 worth of catfish; that's a dollar's worth of catfish to the acre, but they don't say how many catfish are a dollar's worth. If I was going to buy catfish an acre wouldn't hold a dollar's worth, even if I was fond of catfish. This is the first time I ever heard of selling fish by the acre. They say if the lake was drained it would support 1,000,000 people, so an acre will support either a human or a catfish. So the question the state has to decide is what to keep on there, catfish or humans? Up to the present, catfish have won. So if you buy an acre of Lake Okeechobee, your deed will call for one acre and a dollar's worth of catfish. Of course, when you catch him and he is two dollar's worth of catfish, why, then you have to buy another acre or give your neighbor half a catfish. So it looks like a pretty tough job in mathematics down there to divide up your acres, your water, your catfish and your humans.

Who, by the way, wants to eat $1,000,000 worth of catfish? With all the wonderful sea food we have in California, if you offered a man a catfish the criminal courts would have another murder trial on their dockets. Catfish are all right for one who is in a famished or impoverished condition, but for discriminating tastes they are absolutely null and void. Now what is the Humane Society for Catfish going to say about this? And the problem for the investor in buying an acre of this sub-merged land is: "If I drain the water off, the catfish will die; if I leave the water on, the human will drown, so what shall I do?"

FLA.: Lots of people think that Florida is low, but we have a point in Highlands County which is some 310 feet high.

CAL.: Why, Florida is so low it's the only country in the world where you have to climb a ladder to get into the ocean. As for this place in Highlands County they speak of—the Alps of Florida! No native Flori-dian has ever been able to reach the top. When they get up around 200 feet above sea level the altitude gets 'em. About timber line is as far as they can go.

FLA.: The Gulf Stream—you should all know about that. It's the largest river in the world. It's ninety miles wide and we have it. It is the thing that gives us our rare climate.

CAL.: It's all right for Florida to claim the Gulf Stream, but have they spoken to England about it? You know, our seacoast is generally apportioned as follows: American beaches are owned exclusively by millionaires and real-estate operators; then the next three miles belongs to the revenue boats; from the third to the twelfth mile is for the anchorage of our filling stations; and from twelve miles out it is England's. So why does Florida claim the Gulf Stream? Suppose California laid claim to the Pacific trade winds? We wouldn't do it, even if we had Japan's permission. We don't call on the ocean to help us out—we don't take wind from anybody. With movie press agents, Kiwanis, Rotary, Lions, Tigers, and all Sixty-Cent Cold-Potato Luncheon Clubs, we create our own trade winds. And up to now nobody has ever been able to trade wind with us. You Floridians will be claiming the equator next. You say the Gulf Stream gave you your climate. Climate is ours; it is the one thing we will fight for. We have a copyright on it. We are the first ones that ever sold it. No state in the world had thought about advertising climate until California started it. We have spent millions of dollars to make climate our slogan. When you say "Climate" you think of California. Every state has had climate for years, but we are the first ones to conceive the idea of using it. Until our literature fell into your hands you didn't know to spell "climate." I suppose sooner or later that you will be claiming our unusual climate! Try to say that we are not the originators of that! We were the first to discover that when it rains on a day that was advertised to be bright, that was unusual.

FLA.: Florida on the map looks like a finger pointing south. It does. It points to South America, the land of the great development of the next century.

CAL.: Where is the finger pointing? It is pointing to somewhere else. If you will look on the map, it will show this finger of Florida slightly crooked at the end, at a point called Cape Sable, and it is pointing due west to California, the land of the great development of the next century. After all, you can't fool Nature; she knows where to point. Speaking of fingers pointing south, we had one called Lower California. What did we do with it? We gave it to Mexico, because nothing is so useless as a pointing finger. Florida looks like a springboard that points from the land out into the water. But who wants to live on a springboard, where somebody is diving off all the time? California, as you will see by your map, is at the back. It is tall and straight and symmetrical. It's the backbone and the spine of a great country. You can't live without a spine. But a finger means nothing to our national existence. So please never again draw attention to your geographical architecture.

FLA.: We have $15,000,000 worth of fish in the waters bordering on Florida.

CAL.: They're in with fish again! And they have got 'em up to

31

15,000,000 now. Of course, they don't say they have sold these 15,000,000, but they have them there in case some buyer comes along and wants $15,000,000 worth of uncaught fish. It seems they can catch their catfish, but for these others they just give you a floating bill of sale. Now we are going to be honest and tell you that we don't know how many millions of dollars' worth of fish there are in the waters bordering on California. We have heard various estimates by fishermen. Some of the more conservative fishermen estimate them at around $5,000,000,000.

FLA.: We have 500 different kinds of fish. We have the best sporting fish in the world—the tarpon. And if you have ever seen the sailfish, you know what a beautiful fish it is.

CAL.: Now as to varieties, we don't know whether we have 500 varieties or not. We have heard it estimated by several of our trustworthy fishermen that our varieties will run in the neighborhood of a little more than 2,000,000. That is without estimating some of the few odd varieties that were playing around and made themselves hard to count. But we are not like Florida—we don't know exactly. Now we don't know what a fish has to be to be a sport. The tarpon may be a sport in Florida, but he is a moron with us in California. Boy Scouts catch the tarpon with a minnow seine and sell them to the fishermen as bait for the tuna. The tuna is a fish, that if he ever landed in Florida, he would give one yell and have all these other Florida fish climbing coconut trees. And if a Florida fishermen ever hooked one of them, the Gulf Stream would be that fisherman's tombstone. And as for your sailfish, California originated them. Why, on a good sailing day the sky is scaly with them. We have seen the time when you couldn't see the goats on Catalina Island for the sailfish. We cut out all the little ones that couldn't fly very high and shooed them off in the general direction of Florida. So the ones you have there are just kind of a mongrel breed that was littering up a perfect ocean out our way.

FLA.: We are known for our oranges.

CAL.: Why orange, climate, Pickford, California—those four wonderful words can never be dissociated.[2] I will admit there is a bootleg variety of orange that thrives up to the size of a green plum on the banks of your swamps; but as for being called an orange, that is only done, of course, through a sense of humor. We take Florida oranges to California, dry them and use them for golf balls. As for taste, they resemble the green persimmon.

FLA.: Our grapefruit sells for about $10,000,000 a year, and we think it is the best in the world.

CAL.: We use the juice of your grapefruit as a fly spray. We had no idea anyone ate them.

FLA.: Our oranges alone in 1924 brought us in $15,000,000.

CAL.: That would just about pay for the labels on the ones we shipped. Orange County—and it was named because they couldn't seem to get oranges growing good there—after everything was closed up one evening and no one was even thinking about oranges, shipped $5,000,000 worth themselves.

FLA.: We raise $10,000,000 worth of corn. We also raise tobacco. We have 1,000,000 tourists, and it is estimated that they leave $100 apiece with us. That is $100,000,000.

CAL.: Corn? We don't go in for corn. But beans—you take away California's bean crop and the American Army would have to go to feeding their men. As for tobacco, we can't raise as good as North Carolina, and because we can't we don't raise any. No inferior anything for us. It's the best or none at all. Now about those 1,000,000 tourists that leave $100 apiece—why, there are more than that looking for Mary Pickford's house before breakfast every morning along just to attend the Iowa picnic. That many win beauty prizes and are sent there to replace Lillian Gish.[3] Ben Turpin alone has drawn 200,000 cock-eyed guys there. Everybody that has all his front teeth intact and a pair of horn-rimmed glasses comes to replace Harold Lloyd.[4] And as for the Florida tourists leaving $100 apiece, we won't monkey with that cheap trade. It costs our tourists more than $100 just to take a course in scenario writing alone.

ANGRY MOB (interrupting): Just a minute, gentlemen, we want you to listen to us for a while.

CAL. AND FLA.: Who is this that dares interrupt the debate between the two premier states of our great commonwealth? Stop these interruptions! Who is this unimportant upstart anyway?

INTERRUPTER: I'll tell you who we are. We are the state of Oklahoma, and we are what both of you fellows advertise yourselves to be. We are the Chamber of Commerce of Claremore, Oklahoma, the town that needs no introduction to an intelligent audience. We, like the rest of the United States, have sat patiently by for years and listened to you two birds. America couldn't pick up a magazine without looking at a picture of somebody hitting a golf ball in sunny California or balmy Florida. To read the ads, you would think that was the only place golf balls were being missed. You have both howled of your climate till one would think the rest of the states in the Union kept their inhabitants alive by artificial respiration. Now the time has come to revolt. You can push America just so far, even with an ad. We may be a patient race, a tolerant people, and will stand for a terrible lot. We have had things as bad as your menace and lived them down. We remember years ago we went through a siege of cross-word puzzles which littered up our newspapers even worse than your orange groves and your bathing-beach scenes, but we finally turned and solved all those puzzles by throwing them into the ash can. We lived mah-jongg down in one month less than a year, and if you think we are going to spend the rest of our lives looking at the picture of a fat tourist with a rubber fish labeled Tuna or Tarpon, you are overestimating our good nature.

Now, Florida, I know it's going to break your heart to have to listen. You have had the ear and eye of your audience so long that you think they belong to you; and you, California, had the same thing up to the time Florida came along. Then you started weeping some real tears along with your movie glycerin ones, when you had to hear about somebody else. As you know, America doesn't stay on one fad long, and you both have had your chance and you have prospered. Nature, the world and the newspaper have been good to you; but restless America is looking for a new place to fix the tires, and we are here to announce to the half-witted rovers of America that Oklahoma has been designated by Nature as the parking place of the last and greatest boom.

Your two-boy act is finished; you can wash up and go home—where you can spend the rest of your days living on orange juice and throwing rocks at the alligators. We of the Chamber of Commerce of Claremore, Oklahoma, are not the kind of people, like Borah and Jim Reed, who criticize and offer no remedy. Before we dismiss you two states from the tourist time-table we are going to take both of you apart and show what has made you rattle this long. We are going to shoot you through a public clinic and show you how you really stand up when compared to fast company. The truth is, you kids have been so busy fighting between yourselves and trying to shoot each other in the back that you haven't watched the rest of the United States passing by. If you had only looked up you would have noticed who was in the lead. It wasn't a soul in the world but your old Sooner State of Oklahoma.

While you two flea hounds stopped to snap at each other Oklahoma was leading the rest of the pack and gnawing right on prosperity's heels. Old Man Natural Resources is the boy who will eventually settle this argument, and it just looks like the Lord in distributing resources fixed Oklahoma so it would stop all arguments before they started.

Now a golf course in colored photography makes an awful pretty picture, but awful poor nourishment. A bathing beauty in a one-piece suit catches the eye but is not listed in natural resources as a staple. A yacht scene has a certain attractiveness but no particular income attached. But an Oklahoma oil well pumping out the old grease is the thing that bought the white flannel yachting breeches.

We just heard your babbling, telling of what your states contained; now sit there and grit your teeth while we tell you what a real state contains. You kids were all right in the preliminaries, but this is the

34

finals we are in now. As small-timers, you each stopped the show; but up here with us on the big time you will break a leg before you can get a bow. So listen and lament. The test of a state is: What does old Mother Earth underfoot come forth with? Why, we drop more stuff off the wagon going to market than either one of you raises. Your first controversy was about Ponce de Leon. Well, if it is any news to you illiterates, we have dozens of men in Oklahoma living today that knew Ponce de Leon well. These old men remember him as a kid in Florida when they were all searching for the Fountain of Youth together. He died looking for it, while these boys located it at the Radium Wells, which has since been known as Claremore, Oklahoma, the Mecca of the afflicted and the Eden of the home seeker.

In your next prattling of a subdivided mind you state, "Spain sold Florida for five cents an acre." You are right; that is a historical fact, and it is also the first indication we have in history that Spain had no conscience. And as for you, California, Mexico and the United States had a war. We think it was caused by Secretary Kellogg missing one day sending them an ultimatum note.[5] Not to be commanded by America every day made them think we were sore at them. The war was really over the following question: "Who will have to take California?" Mexico won and America had to take it.

These, gentlemen, are the historical facts of how both of you come to litter up our landscape, but look at the difference when we read of the historical acquiring of Oklahoma. When the United States realized what France really possessed in owning the territory embracing Oklahoma, they entered into negotiations for its purchase. But France's minister—whoever he was that day—himself realized what they had within the boundaries of what now embraces Oklahoma. America went so far as to offer beaucoup d'argent—heavy jack—for it. But France also realized that they had a great deal of worthless country on their hands, so they made the following proposal to the United States: "We will sell you Oklahoma; but you must agree to take over—without us paying you for it—Louisiana, Arkansas, Missouri, Iowa, South Dakota, Kansas, Nebraska, and parts of Colorado, Wyoming, North Dakota and Minnesota; and you are also to agree that the purchase is always to be known as the Louisiana Purchase, because if France ever knew we sold Oklahoma, why, another cabinet would fall. But by it being known as the Louisiana Sale they will think we made a good business move, and the Chamber of Deputies will no doubt give us a vote of confidence."

Well, America was tickled to death when they heard we were to get Oklahoma at any price, even if we had had to take Chicago. So out of our promise to France we have always let it be known as the Louisiana

Purchase, but we all know that its real name is the Oklahoma Purchase and the Louisiana Gift.

If our memory serves us right, and it's not too sure in recalling idle chatter, you boys argued something a while ago about seacoast. Say, when the Arkansas, Red River, Salt Fork, Verdigris, Caney, Cat Creek, Possum Creek, Dog Creek, Skunk Branch are all up after a rain, we got more seacoast than Australia; and if you don't think it's real water, try to swim some of them on a horse sometime.

Now as to Florida's Everglades and California's mountains, such things as those are as foreign to us as a crop failure. Every foot of land we have in Oklahoma is tillable. We have neither dredge nor steam shovel. Nature graded our land. You wait for a miracle to aid you, and we've already had ours happen.

Now we come to the catfish. We have such a varmint that infests our waters, but we have never known our food supply to arrive so low that anyone resorted to the catfish for provender. Why, even the peasants in Oklahoma eat goldfish. As to the number of varieties of fish, we couldn't tell you. We, personally, were out fishing one day and our estimate was that there wasn't any; or if there was, we didn't see them. Some of our reliable and conscientious fishermen have estimated it at about 8,000,000,000; so, to be perfectly frank with you, it is somewhere between none and 8,000,000,000.

And as to their names, we don't keep much track of that. We have never got out a Who's Who on fish. Even the mail-order catalogue, which we look to when in doubt on any diplomatic question, fails to list them among the twelve best sellers. A fish is just a fish with us. His build, his literacy or his ancestry never bothers us much. So for queer fish, either on land or sea, we can't compete with either of our ex-illustrious commonwealths.

The transformed Iowan fish that arrives in Los Angeles in answer to a picture post card, with oranges on the trees in the wintertime, is a unique member of the finny tribe which we feel fortunate in not possessing. Nor have we anything to compare with your movie-struck fish; or the film flounder, scenario suckers, Hollywood eels, wall-eyed pikers and your sporting fish, who in Hollywood Saturday nights stay up and go to the second show. As for Florida, the real-estate sharks run in schools, looking to pounce upon the Indiana and Georgia fish called the sucker, who generally migrate singly. So the fair state of Oklahoma goes on record as not being the rendezvous of queer fish. We are a state, not an aquarium. If you want to be a fish, go to Florida or California. If you have any tendencies or aspirations toward being a human, Oklahoma will eventually be your home. Why not now?

Now a few words on your constant howl—climate. California, it took you five years to learn you couldn't live on climate. You have to have some biscuits and molasses to go with it. Florida is just now learning it. Climate is a sales argument, but not a food. Oklahoma is the only one of the three that has an all-year-around climate. Our people don't move with the seasons, hunting a different climate. Our climate changes with our seasons. Why, we throw away more climate that we don't need in one year than you have charged your customers with! We don't sell climate; it goes with the purchase of land, just as the darkness or the light. We don't have to throw in a Gulf Stream or a trade wind or a canceled state income tax or a movie contract or a catfish. There are no remnant sales in Oklahoma. California has to irrigate, Florida has to fertilize. Now it seems hardly right, does it, that the Lord would take both those off an Oklahoman's hands? We don't have to depend on a dam; nor Chile for nitrates. You just throw anything out in Oklahoma and all you have to do is to come back and harvest it.

Pardon us if we laugh when we think of you talking about your geographical position. Why, all you have to do is look at a map and tell that one of you is hanging onto America by your toes and the other by your teeth. You are not really in America; you are just on the ragged edge. You are just the fringe on the coat tail of a well-worn suit, while Oklahoma is the heart, it's the vital organ, or our national existence. Kansas is the appendix; if it ever gets to hurting, we can take it out and never miss it. But Oklahoma! When her economic pulse ceases to beat, America will be laid in the cemetery by the side of Vermont, Maine and Czecho-Slovakia.

As for the distance from New York, that means nothing to us. Let New York estimate their distance from us. We make no effort to toady to their millionaire trade. We raise our own millionaires in Oklahoma.

Now as to oranges and grapefruit. They have caused more talk and given less sustenance to life than anything in the shape of an eatable ever invented. When we raised men in this country, and not golf players, grapefruit was unknown; and today it is as useless as a luncheon club. With us it is considered a kind of an effeminate morning dish. We raise apples in Oklahoma, something that is a recognized food—and not a shower—known and referred to even in Bible times. Peaches, grapes, anything you want, we raise it in abundance.

Corn? When you speak of corn you are talking right up our alley. Why, the way that Florida got that little patch that sold for $10,000,000 was by Oklahoma's corn growing so high that some of the stalks fell over into Florida. We gather our corn in airplanes. Why, our corn last year in Oklahoma ran over 200 gallons to the acre! Our corn keeps the world merry. Most of our hogs are fattened from the mash from the stills; so that's why Oklahoma pork brings more on the market than any other. It's from satisfied and liberty-loving hogs. One Oklahoma ham fattened from still mash runs 3.75 per cent intoxicating. And Oklahoma pigs' feet have been known to do the Charleston right on the dining-room table.

Beans? We have to raise $30,000,000 or $40,000,000 worth of beans to go with our corn, just for succotash purposes, and we are a race of people that don't particularly care for succotash, at that.

Tobacco? We just raise enough of that to last till somebody can hitch up a flivver and go to town.

Tourists? We don't go in for them much. We have figured it out that there is nothing so unproductive as a tourist. He does nothing but use up your roads. He's even buying enough gasoline in his home town to last him through the trip. He just gets in your way on the highways. Pop and hot dogs are the extent of his purchases. The tourists are the modern Coxey's Army of America.[6] But most towns are solving the problem by segregating them off to themselves in free camping grounds. So this is the third of three things we will give you without argument—grapefruit, catfish and tourists.

While you are bragging on your pests, why didn't you, Florida, say something about your mosquitoes? And you, California, your sand fleas? You boys could have been truthful about the number of those things without lying. I know, California, that you claim your fleas have never bitten anyone until after they have bought. And as to the size of your mosquitoes, Florida, our chamber of commerce woke up one morning and the mosquitoes were trying on our overcoats. I know, Florida, you have your coconuts; and know you, too, California, feel envious of them because you haven't got any; but don't worry; you take off the first two syllables and you are even with them.

Oklahoma has no such thing as the idle or unemployed problem, like Florida or California has with its real-estate men. Our chamber of commerce used to go every day, while visiting Miami and Los Angeles, at 12:30 to see them feed the real-estate men.

So, after all, it's the old earth we have working for us in Oklahoma. Some of the ads for the lots you try to sell are bigger than the lots themselves. We produce the oil that runs the cars that you are making payments on. We have coal, oil, gas, wheat, corn, oats, potatoes, cotton, cattle, horses, sheep, hogs—all these are there now. They are not "can be raised" or "will eventually be brought here." They are there now. You know, come to think about it, it is only through generosity that the Chamber of Commerce of Claremore, Oklahoma, allows the name of Florida or California to be associated along with it.

I will admit you have hurt some of the weaker-minded states, but Oklahoma is going out for a different class of citizens; and when Oklahoma arises the whole world listens, because they don't know what surprise she may have in store for them. She has astonished them often, has amazed them many times with her new discoveries, dumfounded them with her intellect, swamped them with her riches, shepherded them politically, been the storehouse of their rations, mothered them spiritually—the mental giant of the constellation of states, the lighthouse of morality, physically a Madonna, the geographical and artistic center of a liberty-searching nation. Never a breath of scandal has touched the fair state of Oklahoma, while crookedness, robbery and even murder have run rampant throughout our fair land. Oklahoma has never even had an assault-and-battery case. She has never lived to see the finger of scorn pointed at her. The United States Constitution, with all its various assortment of amendments, has always been religiously adhered to. Today Oklahoma stands as a model of what George and Tom— Washington and Jefferson—meant the entire nation to be. Every industry establishes a local headquarters where they assemble their clients. And Oklahoma has been chosen the world's round-up grounds from which to make the heavenly flight.

Duck, Al! Here's Another Open Letter

This is another one of those open letters that always litter up Al Smith's mail. Al has got so many open letters that it looks like everybody that writes to him has run out of saliva for the tongue. Calvin is the smartest Guy with those open letters. If they are open, he just leaves the impression they was lost in the mail. You can't smoke Cal out with an open letter. He just thrives on smoke. He won't answer a private letter, much less an open one.

Al, I never saw a man in my life where everybody wants to know or help take care of their business like they do you. You are the champion advice receiver of our day. Now, Al, I have known you for years. I don't mean by that that it's been mutual. But even at that, we been speaking to each other for a good many years. I hung around the old town myself for many a year. I have watched your career. I know the story of your life better than I know the story of Amy's Escape.[1]

I first met you when you was sheriff of N. Y.[2] I thought then that was the highest job of anybody's in the World. Town Marshall of New York, I remember when you quit that, when they made it a straight salary instead of a commission job. Your career has been watched with good wishes from everybody connected with the stage, because you have been the stage's greatest booster among our public men. You seemed to savvy our problems, you spoke our tonguee. It dident get us nervous when you was out in front; it just made us feel good.

Al, your career has been phenomial. You have gone like a fresh opened quart in a crowd. You grabbed the old Empire State, tucked it under your arm and did a Red Grange.[3] Every time they had an election you had the ball. They can't stop you on the home grounds. You are Babe Ruth with a short right-field fence.[4] It's just nothing but the showers for any Guy they send in against you. You can call in your outfielders in your league and set the Republicans down in one-two-three order. You can burn the votes through there so fast on election day that they can't get the bat off their shoulder. They can't produce a man that can even get

---

Saturday Evening Post, October 29, 1927

a foul off you. The man you run against ain't a Candidate; he is just a victim.

You remember the night the Friars Club gave you the big testimonial dinner in N. Y. and I was the one to introduce you. Jimmy Walker was there.[5] That was before either of us ever thought we would be Mayor of a great City.[6] Jimmy was a State Senator and nobody ever thinks a State Senator will ever live it down. Well, I had a lot of my little bum jokes on you because I knew, and we all did, that you was a good fellow and would stand for anything and give back more than you received.

Well, you certainly did come back and knock me over with a beaut. I was joking in my introduction of you about you being an Amateur Actor and took a leading part in all the Theatricals. I said that an Actor was bad enough, but that an Actor that acted for nothing was the last word; that he was a real Ham when a fellow couldent act good enough to get paid for it.

Then when you got up you looked at me and said, "Will calls me a Ham Actor because I acted for nothing. Well, at least my conscience is clear."

You sunk me and knocked the audience right back on their flasks with that one. I figured I would get the worst of it from you, because everybody knows you are mighty handy on your feet when it comes to the repartee. Then do you remember along toward the end of my little tirade I spoke about you owing nothing to Tammany Hall?—that you had outgrown Tammany; that you were the only Tammany product that they could point to Nationally with pride; that as far as National politics were concerned they were a liability instead of an asset to you? Well, you remember my little speech died along about then with a lot of them. There was lots of Tammanyites there. Judge Olivany was right there by us.[7] It was whispered around after the dinner that Will should have stuck to the comedy. But some of the smarter ones told me afterwards that I was right and that it was the truth that hurt.

I was simply trying to pay you the best deserved compliment that I could. Well, if they dident think you was bigger than Tammany that night, they think so now. Now a nomination has passed since then and another one is coming on before either party is ready for it. You are the most talked of man outside Mr. Coolidge in America today. You are out naturally for the Democratic nomination and you will go into the convention with more votes than any other man. You will have the advantage of deligates about like McAdoo originally had over you.[8] But that don't mean you will have enough to nominate.

Now both of you boys feel like you have got a bad deal from the other. He feels if it hadent been for you that he would have been nominated, and you feel if it wasent for him that you would be nominated. Each feels that the other has been wronged, when, as a matter of fact, you have both favored each other up to now. You are in New York.

There is only one trouble with New York, and that is that it is the most self-centered place in the world, outside an Englishman's London. It feels like it's the biggest place in the world and ought to run everything, but it just don't. Politically, nationally, it just looks like Claremore, Oklahoma. You-all there get the wrong prospectus, especially on politics. The men you meet is the big Democratic leaders from all over. They give you glowing accounts, sure they do; you look like their best bet. They tell you what their State will do, but they don't tell you what the Republicans will do.

In the past year I have been all over every State in the Union. I gab politics with every person I meet. Commercial traveling men go round the country swapping funny stories. Now I don't do that. I get all my quiet amusement talking politics and making them think that I am taking it all serious; that's my amusement—watching them be serious about politics.

Now you want the nomination—that's no more than human—and if you get it you will split your party, because unfortunately they are not composed entirely of the brains of our commonwealth. They think that if they elected a wet that the Constitution would be changed the next day and the country would be wet. They don't know that, as a matter of fact, the President never gets what he wants. Pres. Wilson wanted the League of Nations; every President has wanted something that he dident get but Mr. Coolidge, and he was smart enough not to let anybody know what he wanted so they would never know what he had been disappointed over.

Now here is what I am getting at: It's not that you ain't strong all over the Country, Al, for you are; you are the strongest one they got—that is, for a Democrat—and if you was running against Democrats you would beat 'em. But unfortunately in the finals of this somebody has to meet a Republican, and when a Democrat meets him next year it's just too bad. Everybody talks about what's wrong with the Democratic Party. Well, if they will be honest with themselves they will admit there is just one thing wrong with it. They havent got enough voters.

Now why go into a race when you can't win? Politics is the only sporting events in the world where they don't pay off for second money; a man to run second in any other event in the world it's an honor. But any time he runs second for President it's not an honor; it's a pity.

Now, Al, don't let 'em kid you; you can't beat this Guy Coolidge. There has been too much prosperity among big capital to allow a change to be made at this time. As for farmers, there is not enough of them to get anything. The minute they get some bill to want to raise the price of what they raise, they make mad the millions of others that have to buy what they raise. You see, you won't ever remedy that, because there is more people eating than there is raising things to eat.

Coolidge will recommend a bill which he will know that can't be passed, but that will set him in K. O. Besides, Al, your strength hasent been with the farmers in your own State. It's with the people in the cities that don't know whether you shake Alfalfa off the trees or dig it up. They think succotash is one of Burbank's new grafts.[9]

You got the chance of making yourself the biggest man the Democratic Party has housed in many a day. Just frame up a statement something like this—get all the boys in, print it on a slip of paper and just hand it out and don't say a word:

> I, Al Smith, of my own free will and accord, do this day relinquish any claim or promise that I might have of any support or Deligates at the next Democratic Convention. I don't want to hinder what little harmony there is left in the party. I not only do not choose to run, but I refuse to run. But will give all my time and talents to work faithfully for whoever is nominated by the party.
> Alfred E. Smith.

Now, Al, you do that and you will knock 'em for a majority in 1932. You will be the second Thomas Jefferson. You will be so much bigger than the Democratic nominee that it will be embarrassing to both of you. Here is the slick part about it—the mob will think you have done the big generous thing and sacrificed your own welfare to the good of the party. "Gee, that fellow Smith is a real fellow! He is the only real Democrat we have had in years." But in reality you won't be giving up a thing; you will just be saving yourself. Then look where you will be sitting in 1932! Why, they won't even hold a convention; they will nominate you by radio. There would be no way in the world to keep you out; the party would owe it to you.

Now let's just look at the thing and see what four years could do. You know that your Prohibition stand wouldent be any the worse off in four years. It's not going to be an issue this election. Both sides are afraid of it. You watch those platforms and you will see both parties walk around prohibition like a skunk in the road. If you think this Country ain't dry, you just watch 'em vote; and if you think this Country ain't wet, you just watch 'em drink. You see, when they vote, it's counted; but when they drink, it ain't. So that's why the drys will win. If you could register the man's breath that cast the ballots, that would be great. But the voting strength of this country is dry.

'Course the main thing you will be rid of in four years from the vote-getting standpoint will be Calvin—unless they decide to make the position heridary and give it to young John.[10] You will be rid of him without choosing, and by that time the Republicans will have done some fool thing. They have gone along now longer than their average; they are bound to make up for lost time in the next four years. People will be so disgusted with prosperity in the next four years that Ben Turpin could be elected.

You see, here is why Coolidge is unbeatable this year—it's his Cabinet. We will just say, for argument's sake, that the Republicans did run somebody else this time. I bet you they would broadcast the fact that they would, however, retain Mr. Coolidge's present Cabinet. But in four more years they wouldent be in your way. Men like Mellon and Hoover ain't going to stay in there forever. So in '32 you would be rid of all that. The trouble with you politicians is you see, but you don't see far. You wear your reading glasses when you are looking at the future. You got your Putter in your hand when you ought to have your driver.

This should have been done four years ago. It's what you should have done at the convention. You would have been four years ahead. It's what McAdoo should have done then too. You know, Al, it dident take any great foresight to tell before the last election that the Republicans were going to win. A man would have been a half-wit to think the Democrats had any chance. When I think of you two fellows fighting for a nomination that dident mean anything but defeat for either of you, it sometimes makes me doubt whether either one is really qualified for the office.

It was simply a Republican year. You couldent have put on a revival of Thomas Jefferson and got away with it. John W. Davis was one of the most able men in America. Charles Evans Hughes is the ablest. Yet they both were beat.

But we don't elect able men. You think we want to upset the whole idea of Party Government? Now next year is another Republican year. You got no platform. What are the Democrats going to run on? You can't get people to throw another man out just because you all want the job. You got to promise the people something, even if you don't ever expect to give it to them. In four years prohibition might be much more of an issue than it is today—that is, it might be an issue by popular demand, and then you would be sitting pretty.

Besides, you making this move for party harmony might shame some of the rest of the party into doing something to get together and in the next four years be all united. You might round up the West to go in with the South, and then you come in with your Gang from the East, and I tell you the party would be in shape to make a race instead of a sacrifice. And in the meantime you distribute yourself all around over the country and let people see what kind of a Guy you are.

A lot of them think you got stripes and drag a long curly tail. Speak to 'em in person; that's where you shine. The old farmers would fall for you just like the Pants pressers on the East Side. The Radio is all right but it's only good for ones with a Tenor voice. They don't get your personality and that's your long suit.

You see, here is something you never hear about, but it's just what would happen if you were nominated. It would split the ticket. These rabid ones would nominate a dry Protestant in less than forty-eight hours. Now the Democrats ain't hardly got enough to split. But if you give up to them now, they wouldent hardly feel like being so ungrateful to you as to split it in '32.

Now these are just a few things as they strike me. I may be all wet—people that give politics any thought at all generally are. I ain't looking for any appointment. I got to get a few laughs to eke out an existence, and people are just as hard to make laugh under one Administration as the other. It don't make any difference to me who is in. In fact it don't make any difference to 95 per cent of us who is in. The job is really overrated. It's not a Mussolini job by any means.[12]

You see, the old founders of the Constitution made it so it dident matter who was in, things would drag along about the same. I would like to see the Democrats get in four years from now just on account of their perseverance.

Now you listen to your Leaders and they will tell you what you can do. They can come nearer making a showing with you than anybody. But there is no show money in this race. They want you because it won't make them look quite so bad with you nominated.

I will meet you in three or four years from now and I believe you will admit that this was the best plan. If they get you into this, they have kidded you into it, and a New Yorker is supposed to be a wise Guy. A smart Prize fight Manager or a smart race-horse trainer make great prize fighters and great race horses simply by knowing what race to put 'em in or who to fight, and what race to keep 'em out of, and what fighters not to let 'em meet.

I am telling you how you might be President—not just Candidate. And remember, Al, get around and let 'em know you. I have often said you could go into the strongest Clan town, meet all of them and get acquainted, and by the end of the week be elected Honorary Grand Kleagle Dragon.

45

Flying and Eating My Way East

What are you-all doing? Want to take a little trip? What do you say we take a little ride and see some of the country? They say there is nothing that broadens one like travel, so come on, let's go flatten ourselves out a bit. Got to get up early, as we leave at 7:35 in the A.M. 'Course you have been up in a plane lots. No? You mean you never was in one? Well, well, that is interesting. We used to have a old fellow out home at Oologah, Oklahoma, and he had never been on a train. We used to point him out and laugh. I'll bet you would have got a kick out of seeing him, and I know you have laughed many a time at the old story they used to tell about the first train that went down through the mountain country, and the people all standing along on the hillsides.

The brakeman was on top of the box cars, and as the train come by he waved his arms at the people and hollered, "Look out, out there, I'm going to turn it around!"

They all scattered all over the hills; 'course they had never seen one before, didn't know how it worked, or if it worked. But after they had seen a few and saw them go by and knew that they did work, why, they didn't hesitate about getting on them then. And we call them Rubes because they didn't want to ride on the first one they saw.

Where do you want to go? What do you say we go to New York? First thing we got to do is get to the aviation field. Los Angeles is what is called the average American City—that is, the politicians are arguing over where to put their municipal air field. Each politician is trying to sell the ground that belongs to his friends. Who ever thought politics would get into aviation? Say, politics will get into a prairie-dog hole if it can sell the ground the hole is in.

It took us just an hour and a half to drive through the traffic to the field. Ain't autos grand? What would we do without them. If we had had a dirt road, with no expense to the taxpayers, we would have got over there with a horse and buggy in about forty minutes. Well, we are finally there. It's the Western Air Express. They use Douglas planes with 425-horse-power Liberty motors.

Saturday Evening Post, January 21, 1928

Will Rogers prepares for a round-trip, cross-country air-mail flight in
October of 1927.

There's a mechanic in the plane warming it up. The pilot has nothing to do but get in and take his seat. You-all wait here with Mrs. Rogers while I run in and buy my ticket.[1] The fare is $60 to Salt Lake; that's the end of this company's run. Here comes the truck with the mail.

The pilot drives up in his car. His wife is with him and he has the cutest twin kids. They have come to see that he got through the dangerous part of his journey O. K. His wife seemed relieved that he made every grade crossing safely. I bought a flying suit; it's a leather affair, sort of a cross between pajamas and bib overalls. The pilot, Jimmy James, tells me he doesn't think I will need it, that it is very warm.[2] Well, that spoiled my whole day, for that's all I was going for, was to get to wear the suit. I felt as bad as the old-fashioned motorist would have felt if you had taken away his linen duster and his gauntlet gloves. You know, they used to wear goggles in those days for autos, too. That was to keep the runaway horses out of your eyes.

It's an open plane. I'm in the front cockpit and the pilot behind in the other. The only way you can communicate with him is when you land, or by passing written notes. There is so much mail that the place where I am is being packed with it too. I cautioned my wife to be careful of the traffic going home and she said she would. I told her she had better wire me at Salt Lake and let me know if she made it O. K. Jimmy is in giving her a last warming up. She is roaring like a Boulder Dam senator. It's 7:35. They pull the blocks out from under the wheels, a mechanic grabs a wing and helps pull it around, Jimmy gives her the gun and we're going across the ground like a scared rabbit. Did you feel it when we left the ground? I didn't.

We are leaving the city of Lost Angeles, the exclusive home of the Eighth Art, the ultimate home of the performer and the reformer. We are headed to New York by airplane. I had a friend left last night on the crack train for the East. He is an awfully busy fellow and was in great hurry. He had to get to New York and attend to some business, get back home here just as quickly as he can. So he left last night. It's a little foggy as we leave, but that's very unusual here in California. We seldom ever have fog—pardon me while I grin.

We are going over the edge of Pasadena, the old-time home of the retired millionaire. It had quite a vogue before Beverly Hills corraled Mary Pickford. The mountains are on our left; in fact we are just skirting along the side of them. There's Mt. Wilson right there. We can see the great government observatory. They are the old boys that tell you where Venus will be 11:45 P.M. Thursday, February the ninth, but they can't tell you where a single one of Hollywood's stars will be any hour of any day.

Oh, there's old Baldy, the mountain we point out that has snow on it. When the Easterners come out and say, "Oh, this climate is fine, but I do

48

so love to see the snow in the winter. I do miss it here," we say, "Lady, come here. Look right over there. See that snow-capped mountain. That's old Baldy."

They get one look, we get out the pen and show them where to sign, and the lot goes into escrow. We take a substantial-enough first payment down on it that should these unusual fogs obstruct their view and she couldn't get a peek at old Baldy, we would still be in the clear financially.

We are flying high now, for we have to get over the mountains pretty soon. Yes, we are getting close to old Baldy now. I turn my head and shout back to Jimmy and point at the same time. "Baldy?" He can tell what I mean and he nods, saying, "Yes, it's Baldy." But wait a minute; we are getting right near it. We are high and most on a level with it.

What is that stuff? Why, that isn't snow! It's some substance that looks like snow. Well, bless my old movie education! If I had never worked in the movies, I never would have been able to have noticed it. I doubt if Jimmy knows it yet. My Lord, don't ever let it get out among the real-estate men, but old Baldy ain't got a snow cap on. Why, you old reprobate, Baldy! Now we are closer and closer.

Can you beat these Californians for injuenuity? Got to be ingenious to spell that so people will know what you mean. If they haven't taken the top of that poor old mountain and covered it over with this preparation that we use in the movies that looks like snow! It's really a kind of salt. Well, sir, they have spread that over the top of this peak.

I always wondered why no more and no less snow always got up there. It always looked like the same amount. But that's what it is. It's that old crystal movie snow that can exist in the Mojave Desert in July. Charlie Chaplin mushed his dogs through it two summers and two winters right in Hollywood while he was making that picture called the Gold Rush.[3] The dogs like to died from the heat and old age as they plowed through this Hollywood desert. In fact it photographs better than snow; it looks more like snow than snow.

Talk about going to Alaska for scenes, why, Alaska comes to Holly-wood in barrels! We are crossing right over. It's so hot I have to take off my helmet. How the men kept from suffocating from the heat that put it here I'll never know. Now we are crossed over and on the opposite side.

Get this: There's no snow. They only put it on the side that shows. It's a snow-capped peak to Los Angeles, but it's just an old bare mountain peak to the residents of Victorville, on the other side. Now we are going over Victorville, where we all used to come to take our Western pictures because there was a good hotel there. I made one right down there on that ranch that's under us now. Well, the same ranch we all used.

I'll never forget that picture I made there. I was supposed to get on a bucking horse in a corral and he was supposed to buck out of the gate

49

and down to the creek, where he was to throw me off into the water. Then the leading lady was supposed to come up and see me as I was crawling out of the water, and I was to register embarrassment and try to conceal my wetness at the same time. It was in the wintertime when we took it. The fellow that wrote this little byplay in the scenario did so in a nice warm dry room.

Well, I got on the horse and got almost to the gate, when he bucked me off. We caught him and did it over again. And the next time I stayed with him until he got out of the gate and that was all.

The director said, "That's no good. You'll have to try it again. You are supposed to stay on until you get to the creek and then get bucked off."

I says, "Say, listen, if you want me to do this scene, you get a corral that's nearer the creek; or better still, find some creek that's nearer a corral." So I'll never forget that ranch.

We are heading out across the bare old hills for Daggett and Barstow. There ain't much to see, but the coloring in the hills looks mighty pretty. The old ship is going along just as steady as a rock; can't feel any vibration at all. The air is mighty smooth.

He punches me and hands me a note. Let's look at it and see what he says: "The famous Calico Range is the low rough spots on the left. After a rain you can see all the colors of the rainbow in the soil. That's the Union Pacific coming down from Salt Lake over on our left, and on our right is the Santa Fé from the East. They come together and both use the same tracks into Los Angeles down through the Cajon Pass."

Well, now that is fine. We know just where we are. Not that I cared much, but it did relieve me to know that the pilot did. You know, a passenger can be lost all the time and not know where he is, but it's when he feels that the pilot is lost, then it becomes embarrassing. . . . Wait, here's another note:

"Here is some figures that might be interesting to you, Mr. Rogers. I have read all you have written about aviation and I appreciate it, and want you to know what our company is doing. We have been in operation one year and a half; traveled 650,000 miles; only had four forced landings, which were quickly repaired and ships flown on to destination; not even a mashed finger or accident to passenger or employe; only failed to leave Los Angeles once, and that was last winter during heavy rains and storms; not a train left there on a single railroad that day. We started out this line with only twenty pounds of mail; today we have 550 pounds on board. Only one replacement of personnel and that was of minor importance.

"If you ever write anything on this, as you sometimes do, please give credit to the ground crew. Nobody ever says anything about them, and if it wasn't for them we couldn't have done all this.

"We have a very wonderful ground crew. Successful operation depends upon skilled workmen. The ship you are in now was in the Los Angeles auto show, February, '26, when new. Also in the show of '27, with 75,000 miles to her credit. Today (over) it has 135,000 miles and will go in next spring's show with close to 180,000. We have carried over 1000 passengers."

Now wasn't that a nice note? And it gives us a kind of added confidence in our trip when we know what their record is. I was just a-thinking, there's a fellow that's proud of his job. He is good at it because he is pleased and—well, I can't say what I want to, but I am going to give Brisbane the idea and let him write an editorial on what makes men successful is to be pleased with their jobs.[4] I got the idea, but I'm shy on words to fill it out with.

Here's Jimmy with another note. He must be running this ship with his feet.

"We are making pretty good time now. Of course, over the mountains, where we climbed to 8000 feet, that slowed us up. But we are doing quite a bit better than 100 miles an hour now. We will cross the line out of California into Nevada in about ten minutes, and it's not uncommon to get a pretty big bump as we cross the line, so kind of watch out. (over) That's one of my little bum jokes about the bump on the line."

But the funny part about it was that it was no joke at all. He was right. The plane took a sudden drop the minute we got out of that California atmosphere. We had been buoyed along on that conversational air out there. Even the temperature of the air changed. It had been hot all through California right up to the line, and then when we got into Nevada it cooled off. It just felt like air that hadn't been inhaled and exhaled as much. Say, this is great air right here in Nevada. Seems like a fine climate too. Wonder why these people don't sell it. . . . Here's another note:

"This is the last note I will trouble you with before reaching Las Vegas, Nevada, where we come down for gas. If you don't want to be bothered with them just let me know there. Death Valley is on our left; the real heart of it is just over that ridge. Remember reading about the movie actress and the aviator that was lost in the desert? Well, right down there was where they were supposed to be lost. I guess they were, the papers printed it, but it's pretty hard to land an airplane without tracks. We will come down in about twenty minutes. You can have a stretch and walk around while we are gassing up."

I then passed him back a note asking if that was the aviator that was supposed to have the lion in the plane.

He answered back, "No, this one didn't have a lion; he had a girl. You don't suppose us pilots are crazy enough to get lost with a lion, do you?"

51

Here she is, a very pretty little town that is a real oasis of several thousand people. They got plenty of water and trees right out on the edge of the desert. Jimmy is bringing her down. There we are, a real three-point landing. She is a sandy field and we are taxiing up to the little oil station.

"Hello, Jimmy, how they coming?"

"I'm a little late. We had a head wind over Cajon and a three-quarter one on in. If we get this all the way it will hold us back."

"Say, Jimmy, I hear Wallace Beery is coming up on tomorrow's ship, going to Chicago."[5]

Jimmy walked around near him to where he was loading the gas and I purposely walked away, as I thought he might have something to whisper that would be embarrassing for me to hear. Jimmy whispered to him, and the first words I heard was: "Who?" Then Jimmy rewhispered. Then I plain heard, "Never heard of him."

Then I piped up, "What's the name of this damn town?"

But nevertheless it's a dandy little city and you'll hear much of it, for it's only fifteen or twenty miles from the site of the great Boulder Dam that will eventually be built when the Government takes it over and tells each state what they get instead of what they want. It has to be built, for the Lord has already done most of the work, and this very Las Vegas is the place that will be the headquarters of all the work and workmen. You will see this name in many a date line in the next few years.

It's about ten o'clock and we've come over a couple of hundred miles, but we've got about 400 yet to do before we reach Salt Lake.

I says, "What are we waiting on?"

Jimmy says, "The fellow with the mail. Here he comes now."

Jimmy took it and stuck it into the ring of the lock on one of the mail sacks. We taxied her out and turned back into the wind and here we go. Over the town and out toward the mountains. We can see the outlines of the Colorado River away over on our right. She's a beautiful day and we are flying high. I was just sort of dozing off to sleep about an hour later when Jimmy punched me in the back with another note.

"This is the Escalante Desert. It's just flat and level like this for 175 miles. We can set the plane down and taxi it along for the whole distance. It's apparently worthless only for sheep. Those black dots on the ground are ant hills, great big red fellows. We might see some wild horses; we generally do."

Now that's mighty nice, and see how it helps out on a trip like this. What do you get on a train?

"Tickets! Hey, wake up! Where's your ticket? What's the idea you didn't have this ticket validated? Change at the next stop."

As I was about to doze off to sleep I got to looking at those mail bags stacked around my feet. I wanted to read 'em. Then I thought what's the use. I know what they are anyhow. It's real-estate and oil circulars, with air-mail marks on them so as to make people take notice of them. But I will just read you a few of the letters offhand. Here is the condensed contents of twelve that are from the movie producers back to the head offices in New York:

"It looks like a great picture. If we will just spend another $200,000 on it, it will be. It's a fair picture as it is, but send $200,000 more and that will make it great."

Now we'll read some of the letters from those that foolishly believes somebody when they told them they looked like Gloria Swanson, or that they were twice as funny as Charlie Chaplin.[6] There was 867 that read:

"Haven't had a chance yet, but if you can just send more money, feel certain they will eventually see their mistake and take me on soon. I saw Mae Murray on the street the other day.[7] Just think what it will mean when I get my chance, and then have you and Pop and all the tribe, and our own cars and have a chauffeur. Haven't much time. Am expecting a call. Send money either by telegraph or air mail. I am more confident than ever. Yours."

About 411 read as follows:

"Ma, see if you can't get Dad to dig once more. I'll pay him back and more. I have seen all these so-called comedians out here. Passed Buster Keaton right on Sunset Boulevard.[8] Went right up close to him. He didn't make me laugh. Why, Ma, you know yourself that I've got more laughs at home at parties than these fellows will ever pack into a feature. It's pull that keeps them there. Tain't talent they want. It looks like I'll get in soon. Make Dad dig. He's an old fogy and thinks I don't know anything. You could cop it from him and send it yourself. Do this, Ma, and you and I will wear diamonds. Your funny old son, Happy."

Say, I'm hungry; it must be near lunchtime. Which way is the diner? Betty fixed me up some sandwiches. They are in my grip in here; it is packed under the box of movie film. They are sending all the finished pictures by air express now. If we are wrecked, look what the world will miss seeing. In order to satisfy public demand they are being rushed by air mail. If I had a projection machine I could run them while we are going.

Never mind, we know what they are without looking at them. There is five war pictures and three Bible ones. They are all doing those now. There is no royalty to pay on either the Bible or the war. Will Hays looked up the copyright law on both events, handing down a decision. We will have to have another war pretty soon. We will have about pictured this one to death.

Here is the grip. Pajamas. I guess she thought I would take off my

53

clothes over Wyoming tonight, brush my teeth, put the cat out on the wing and wind the speedometer and have the pilot come over and tuck me in. Lord, here is a suit of clothes! I guess she thought I would dress for gas at Omaha at one o'clock tonight. Shirts, shirts, underwear. I'll change over Chicago in the morning if all the bandits miss me. Neckties—there is nothing like having plenty of neckties when you are over Nebraska at night. We may have a forced landing and what would it be without a fresh tie?

Here are the sandwiches. She had 'em hid as usual. Just another woman. She thought I couldn't find them, but I fooled her. If they are all cheese and roast beef, the ants will go to war over them. Oh, look what a mess of junk there is here! She had read about what Lindy took to Paris so she has made a sucker out of his commissary department.[9]

"Here, Jimmy, grab an armful of this before it blows back to Los Angeles."

Here is the leavings of the Rogers household for days. Two ·whole chickens and a ham as an appetizer. Here is a whole pie and a chocolate cake. Flying high and eating pretty. Note from Jimmy says:

"We are going out of Nevada and into Utah."

Brigham, I envy you.[10] I only got one; the law and looks kinder slow me up matrimonially, but I got to give you credit; you sure did pick a fine country to fly over.

As I live, here is a bottle full of coffee. I hope it don't keep me awake tonight, as I want to see Iowa so I can tell Long Beach what the old home site looks like. . . . Here comes news from the rear! It's a greasy note:

"That's Zion National Park on our left. It's becoming one of our great show places. Also Bryce's Canyon. We might see the down plane from Salt Lake any time now."

Then come a punch and a shout from Jimmy:

"There he is away down low! Let's go down and see him."

Oh, boy, he has shut off his motor; it feels like we are dropping. That made me stop eating for a minute. I hope we do pass him and not light on him. . . . Hey, look out there! Not so close! How can you tell what he is going to do?

We passed so fast it might have been Lindbergh or Coolidge piloting it for all I could tell. I got right back to my regular business of this trip, which is eating. I munch along on some fried ham with raw sliced onions on 'em till I get the following: "Wild Horses!"

And sure enough, there they were, but they didn't seem afraid of this plane. I guess that's about all they see and they had got used to it. They weren't quite as pretty as they are pictured in the wild-horse moving pictures. I didn't see any stallion standing on a hill on guard. And there wasn't a one in the bunch that was worth breaking.

"On your right is Lake Utah, a freshwater lake, 30 miles from Great Salt Lake, which is 25 per cent salt. Lake Utah drains into the Great Salt Lake by way of the River Jordan, practically the same arrangements as they have in the Holy Land. 30 minutes more to go."

There is Salt Lake City away over there nestled up against those mountains. I tell you those old-timers had an eye to beauty when they settled. Don't she look pretty? And those big wide streets. They was made for ox teams so as to have room to turn around in. Too bad Philadelphia and Boston had nothing but a team of Quakers or Pilgrims to turn around.

Oh, I remember this field. I flew here last winter in a snowstorm from Elko, Nevada, with a pilot named Williams.[11] I want to see him and thank him. He is a real aviator. He circled in those mountains for hours when you couldn't see fifty feet ahead of us, but he made it in here.

"Nice landing, Jimmy. It was a fine trip. May catch you going back in a day or two."

"We didn't make such very good time. That head wind held us back, but we didn't do bad. There's your plane you leave in."

There's the one that just brought the mail from Frisco. Now we change lines. The mail contracts is let from New York to the Coast in three contracts. One from New York to Chicago, one from there to Salt Lake, and the Western Air Express to Los Angeles. This is the Boeing Line now.

"We have a box of lunch here for you, Mr. Rogers, and a vacuum bottle of coffee. You've got time to eat it here while they are changing the mail to your plane, or we will put it in the cabin for you to have on the trip. Come over to the office and get your ticket."

I give them a check for $142 that covers the fare from Salt Lake to Chicago. Understand, this is no special trip at all. It's only the regular trip on the regular mail planes that leave every day and that anyone can walk down and pay their fare and make it. It's around $200 from Los Angeles to Chicago. Less than double what your railroad fare and meals and sleeper would be. Now this plane and this pilot is going to take us from Salt Lake to Cheyenne, Wyoming. Received this message at Salt Lake from manager of the line we had just come over:

"Hope you had good trip. Your pilot, Jimmy James, holds record from Salt Lake to Los Angeles, four hours and five minutes, over six hundred miles. Our radio is there on the field if you want to send messages anywhere."

Well, we have been here about twenty minutes and are about ready to go. . . . Oh, here's a message from my wife:

"Arrived home safely. Betty."

I am introduced to a gentlemen, a Mr. Brady.[12] He is the head of the

Labor Bank in New York. He has been out to the big Labor Convention in Los Angeles and has come in on the plane from Frisco and was going to Chicago. These are inclosed planes and have a little compartment that seats two people side by side kinder like seats in a day coach, only not quite so wide. The pilot is out in an open cockpit behind us. We can't talk or communicate with him, and I knew the note writing would be out, and I am going to miss it. It is nice and comfortable in here; little windows on each side; if you want more air you can slide them back.

We're off! It took quite a run. We have lots of mail. Not only from Los Angeles and Frisco but the other line that runs out to Boise, Idaho, to get Borah's daily instructions to Coolidge. We had about 1500 pounds on there besides this Labor leader and this Labor shirker on board. It's mighty pretty, as you keep climbing higher, as you go over Salt Lake City and out over the Government fort. You see, we got to get some altitude, for we got to hop over these mountains right now, and not go away around them by Ogden, but just stick her nose in the air and ski over the top of them.

Now when I told you this seat was narrow, I didn't just put that in there to take more words. It is either terrible narrow or this old Labor boy keeps spreading out. He is a big husky thing. 'Course these Labor leaders don't do any laboring after they are able to lead. But there was a time during this guy's life that he had done some laboring, and whatever it was, it fully developed him. I would turn my shoulders crosswise and still he would spread over onto to my side.

It is mighty pretty this evening. We had left Salt Lake along about three and are about to make a stop at Rock Springs, Wyoming, to take gas. Saw lots of bands of sheep being driven into Salt Lake to market. It was just starting to get dusk as we saw the first beacon light on what looked like a prairie, but as we passed it, it was up on a high rim with a valley below it, and there was hundreds of little lights around a field. That must be the airport at Rock Springs. It isn't dark enough to need them, but they had 'em lighted. We swung around over the hangar and away down and then turned and made a dandy landing. This pilot's name was, I think, Frank Yaeger, who is taking us from Salt Lake to Cheyenne.[13]

We got out to stretch and look around. There wasn't much there but this old hangar. They had an extra ship in it in case of emergency. I noticed that when the pilots and the men are filling the tanks they all had pistols strapped on 'em. I don't know whether that is an army regulation in regard to the mail or whether they had heard about this banker that was on there with me.

We took a terrible long run to get out of there, as the pilot said it was a bad field to get out of. We made it fine and it is just getting dark. Now I start my first experiences of night flying in America. I had flown at night in Germany, but never over here. We commenced seeing these revolving beacon lights; they are placed about every 25 miles, and lots of them have a row of little lights around what kinder looks like the size of a baseball park. Well, those are the ones that have emergency landing fields. These boys can land at those in the dead of night with no fear of danger. You know, a lot of those lights operate themselves. They have a kind of windmill arrangement that generates its own power and kind of a thermostat thingamajog that turns them on when night comes and off when daylight comes. Nobody goes out to them at all. Some of them have keepers that live in little houses. You never thought you would see lighthouse keepers clear across our Western plains, did you? They have tanks of gas there in case of a forced landing for fuel.

It looks mighty pretty. It is a beautiful night. Then I thought we better get back to the business in hand, which is eating. He had one of those box lunches and his bottle of coffee. So we make our spread. We cleaned up these two boxes and then I remember that the old Rogers knapsack wasn't near empty, so we dug it out and kinder topped it off with some of my homemade.

Well, all this eating is mighty fine, but it has its drawbacks. The more he ate, the more he expanded. Finally I thought I would have to go out on the wing and do a little wing walking and have a chance to spread myself and relax. The specifications in these planes might call for two people, but not one prosperous Labor leader and a well-fed actor at the same time. It was either laid out for two of Singer's Midgets, or one frail woman accompanied by a male contortionist.[14]

Every little while we would pass a train, creeping and crawling and twisting around. We were due in Cheyenne around eight o'clock. The only friend along the line I had wired was Charley Irwin.[15] If you have ever been to the Cheyenne Frontier Days Show, you know Charley. You remember, the Grand Stand would be packed and there was another crowd riding up and down on the race track. Well, that last crowd I spoke of was Charley. Or if you ever went to Tia Juana and couldn't see the races, that was Charley. Coffroth finally built him a pen and put him in the middle of the center field.[16] He weighs 423 pounds in his stocking feet, barefooted, with not an ounce of superfluous clothes on.

You have heard of a man that raced a stable of race horses. Well, Charley races a pastureful of 'em. Outside of the first three in a race, he owns all the others. His daughters were the first great girl riders, and I am sorry to say, started the so-called vogue of Cow Girls. The trouble is that most of them never saw a cow and are not girls any more.

One of the prettiest sights I ever saw is the field at Cheyenne as we circle over it. Here is the town all lighted up and then off near it is this immense big field with a row of electric lights clear around it, and big flood and arc lights playing on the field, and all the headlights from the automobiles shining on the field. Frank sets her down like a real mail pilot can do.

He leans over and says, "We made pretty good time, considering we had a head wind practically all the way."

I started climbing out, and then all at once it got dark. It was old Charley standing between me and the flood lights. He and his girls, and some friends, along with ex-Governor Carey, were there to see me.[17] They have a big lunch fixed for me to eat in their car while they are changing the mail over to a new plane. But I tell 'em I will take it with me; that I think I might stand it a few minutes longer before eating. We had a fine visit, and then they holler, "All aboard!"

That stop taught me a lesson. No matter what happens, it might be worse. Here I am kicking on the size of this Labor leader, and suppose I had drawn Charley for a companion. I would have just rode on one prong of the propeller.

A well-lighted field at night, with planes coming in, just reminds you of a carnival, or Coney Island. It's a real kick landing on a real lighted field at night. It makes you feel like we are really getting somewhere with our aviation. There is not much kick coming into a depot. All you see is the sides of the other cars, but when you swoop down out of the darkness onto all this flood of light and efficiency—well, I will have to get somebody to write an editorial about that.

They introduce me to our next pilot; I think his name is Allison.[18] They say he is one of their cracks. I know he is; they all are. What a great bunch of men we got in this mail service! You know, I am at heart a coward. I am scared of everything, but I just got so much confidence in these pilots that I just crawl up in there like a baby crawling up into its mother's arms. She could walk into the fire with him, but that baby knows she won't.

Why, these fellows are the most careful ones in the world. They have all flown long enough to know the danger of it. Do you think they are purposely taking a chance with their lives? I always figure their lives are worth more than mine. I've lived mine and had my fling, while most of theirs is in front of them. I don't advise flying with anybody that happens to have a thing that is shaped like an airplane. But I do advise with the utmost confidence anyone flying with our real recognized passenger lines.

There is guys trying to fly planes in this country that couldn't keep a kite up on a windy day, and they have some 1910 cars with wings fastened on 'em and a propeller where a bumper ought to be. But these real boys, they have half a dozen different things up their sleeve to do in case of any kind of danger. I will get in one and start for the Fiji Islands with an Army, Navy or Mail pilot if he says he thinks he can make it.

Lindbergh is a great flyer and he come from a great school. The Army, Navy and the Mail are our three sure-fire branches. It's not only the men, it's the equipment they use that makes 'em safe. As the old pilot we had away back there this morning said, "Don't forget the ground men."

Well, we must quit raving and get back to eating and flying. We take a long run, but we got a real field to do it on. We are heavier now. We have the mail from a feeder line down to Denver, then Cheyenne's post-card quota. We are off to Omaha, with a stop for gas at North Platte, Nebraska. We will change planes and pilots again in Omaha. Then from there on in to Chicago.

Well, we didn't do so bad in Cheyenne. The company had us two nice box lunches in the cabin, and in addition a boxful of Y6 pullets Mrs. Irwin had fried up.[19] You should have seen that old walking delegate leave that regulation box lunch and circle around these breasts and wishbones of these Wyoming Rhode Island Reds. I didn't begrudge him the chicken, but I did the space. I had to eat to hold my own.

I know Lindbergh broke a lot of records; the greatest one is that he is the only man ever took a ham sandwitch to Paris, and they also claim he made the whole trip on half a sandwich. I have killed a whole ham and six chickens, an armful of pies and cakes and a clothes basket full of odds and ends and haven't got to Omaha yet, and I had a good breakfast at home this morning before leaving. I could never make a long-distance flight; they couldn't carry enough grub to keep me.

Well, there is not much happens only steady eating until we reach North Platte, about 250 miles out of Cheyenne. We got our gas; they have no letter today, so we are off for Omaha, another 200 or 300 miles. It was away along after midnight when we got there, and I had been doing a pretty fair job of sleeping when the hunger pains didn't keep me awake. Allison brings her down like a bird.

"We made pretty good time considering we were bucking a head wind every mile of the trip."

We are happily informed that there are lunches in the other plane for us, so it looks like our starvation period is at an end. We draw as our pilot I. O. Biffle.[20] He is an old-timer and quite a character, and I think he is the one other pilots in Chicago told me that first taught Lindbergh to fly.

We are out of Omaha and I should judge it is about two o'clock A.M. We are heading for Chicago on our last lap of this company's mail contract. We are going to stop for gas in either Iowa City or Des Moines. It's almost breaking day as we pull into Iowa City. We passed the Des Moines field, saw it all lighted up, and there was a fog on at Iowa City. Then Biffle started raving at the man that had misinformed him about the fog. He could have got gas in Des Moines had they told him of the fog at Iowa City. You see, they have radio and weather reports available all the time.

Well, it's a small field down near a river, and the fog is settled in there, and Biffle was afraid, with the heavy load he had to take off with, he couldn't get altitude enough to clear the telegraph wires. You can't see 200 feet, and old Biffle is sure balling them out. No wonder Lindbergh got good training.

We waited, and finally it commenced to clear. That only shows you how careful they are. We made it away fine, but quite a while late, and have a nice daylight trip into Chicago. We are here about 7:30 or eight o'clock. Biffle says:

"We had a tough head wind all the way, and that kind of held us back. But we didn't do so bad, as it was."

We land out at Maywood Field on the West Side. We are changing now to the National Air Transport, which operates from Chicago to New York. All the planes on this line from Salt Lake have been, as I said, inclosed. They are Boeing-made planes, made in Seattle, and they use the Wasp engine made in Hartford. It has proved tremendously satisfactory to them and they are having bigger ones made that will enable them to carry four or six passengers. They will be 500 or 600 horse power. They have never had any accidents and have some bad country to fly over.

Now we get the open planes again. Douglas, the same as we had yesterday to Salt Lake.

Well, here is some nice coffee and breakfast that certainly is welcome after this day and night of fasting. My broad-shouldered friend is going to Washington in a government plane and I am the only person in Chicago smart enough to fly to New York today.

Now let's kinder check up on this trip and see where we are. Left Los Angeles just a little over 24 hours ago, gone pretty near 2000 miles. I wonder where my friend is that was in such a hurry to get to New York that he left a night ahead of me. He has been gone now two full nights and one day, and as I look at his time-table, he hasn't got to Albuquerque yet. They are hollering, "All aboard!"

I must get this little bit of breakfast eaten. I slept pretty good last night, and feel fine this morning, and will be in New York for dinner tonight if something don't happen.

But something did happen. I had a forced landing in the Alleghanies, but I am not going to tell you about that now. I am not tired of this trip, but I am tired setting here pecking away. So I am going to make a forced landing on this little old typewriter until next week. Takes longer to tell about one of these trips than it does to make it.

Bucking a Head Wind

Well, let's see. I left you in Chicago last week, didn't I? Well, if any of you are living yet, we will drop back and pick you up. Wait a minute, before we get through Chicago, have any of you got an English name? Do you use English mustard?

I don't want to get into any trouble with my old friend Bill Thompson.[1] He and I are both uninformed cowboys, and he and I have agreed that he is to keep King George out of Chicago and I am to ride herd on Rupert Hughes and see that he don't land in Beverly Hills, either personally or in the library.[2] Even if he finds a library in Beverly, I won't let him park his propaganda there. He and King George are not going to make a sucker out of our old original George. Washington might have taken a nip now and again, but at least he never voted against it anyway.

But come on, these shots around this town are getting on my nerves. I am tired seeing these tremendous funerals passing with bandits in $20,000 coffins. He's got to be a pretty high-class bandit in Chicago in order to pay for his casket.

Let's see, when I left you last week I was having breakfast. Well, I am just about through now and they have changed the mail over to the other plane. For the benefit of those who weren't fortunate enough to get one of last week's periodicals, I will explain the scenopsis of the preceding chapters. I left Los Angeles yesterday morning at 7:30—that was Tuesday morning. Now it's Wednesday morning, just twenty-four hours later, and I am leaving Chicago for New York. Now that's all there was to last week's installment. And if you don't want to read this one I will give you a synopsis of it.

I go pretty near to New York by airplane today, finish by train and then back out tomorrow and straight on through to Los Angeles, where I arrive day after tomorrow evening. So that's all there is to this. So turn right on over to your love story. If you don't want to read it in THE POST, wait a few weeks and you will see it at your favorite theater. But by all means don't read it and then go see it too, for you will never recognize it.

Saturday Evening Post, January 28, 1928

You know, come to think of it, I believe I've hit on a great idea right here, by telling people in a couple of lines what the story contains. I think a lot of us will make friends with everybody that just reads the synopsis. So from now on, at the head of all of my articles, I will tell what's in 'em, in a few lines—maybe one.

Now I've forgotten this pilot's name and I want to apologize to him. I shouldn't have, for he brings me back tomorrow night from Cleveland. I believe it is Burnsides or Neville.[3] We have a tremendous load of mail and we are off. The fare I just gave them for this end of the ride is about $200. That seems a little high in comparison to the other end, as it is only that much from Chicago clear to either Los Angeles or Frisco. That makes the whole one-way fare of the trip $407—not more than twice what you would pay on a train, including four days and nights, berth and food.

This is not special, just a regular mail plane that goes at this hour every day. Then tonight there is another leaves here that has the last mail and is in New York in the morning for the earliest delivery, and the same back from there. This is the only line I know of that has a double schedule every day both ways. We are a little late. It must be about 9:30, but it won't take us long to wing our way to Cleveland. There is no stop between here and there.

If you don't think old Chicago is big, just fly around the edges and look her over. It's a beautiful day, and as we get out over Indiana those well-kept farms look mighty pretty. There looks like a farmer on every corner of a 160 acres. I hope we fly over Culver Military Academy. I might see my boy walking guard there.[4] We are going over South Bend. You can just see those old Indiana farmers down there kinder resting on their plow handles and thinking about politics. They don't care what corn or wheat makes to the acre. All they want is more elections, and more plotting to the election.

Now we are in Ohio and headed for Cleveland. Ohio has Donahey for the Democrats and Nick for the Republicans.[5] Either one of them has got a chance of going over. I wish they would nominate both of them. Indiana hasn't much of a chance. Indictments are thicker than voters over there.

Here we are at the field before you know it. I hadn't even see Cleveland yet. I wonder what the depot is doing.[6] They think it will make the town, when, as a matter of fact, it will only encourage people to leave there.

"Nice landing, buddy, nice landing."

The pilot said, "Thanks. We'd 'a' made better time if we hadn't had a head wind all the way over. But we did pretty good considering everything."

Will Rogers aboard an air-mail plane during his unprecedented cross-country trip in October of 1927.

Well, I thought it looked strange. There didn't seem to be much activity around like at the other airports. I didn't see any plane with an engine all warming up. I got out and went into the office and says, "When do we leave?"

"Leave—leave? Who—when—what?"

"Why, we haven't had anything through here either way from New York since Sunday night." This was Wednesday noon. "It's the first time we have been held up all year, but things are very bad over the mountains. There is a dense fog and low-pressure area just blocked in there and it seems mighty slow moving."

"Well, you mean to tell me we won't get out for New York this afternoon? I sure would like to go through if it's possible."

Well, we moved over to the map on the wall that has all the latest weather reports. I could see something laying over the East. I couldn't tell whether it was Low-Pressure Area or just plain rain and storms, or scandal. He called in Brownie—Henry J. Brown.[7] He was on the list as the first pilot out and had been since Sunday night. There is another guy that does nothing but take care of the weather. He was getting reports all the time. Brownie had a conflab with him and said it seemed to be lifting in some quarters. He said we would have lunch and then see what would happen.

Well, I hadn't had anything since nine and it was then about one— only a snack that was left over from Breakfast that I brought along and eat on the way over. We had lunch and then we stood around and the pilots would do some ground flying. There was a whole band of them there. They said it would be pretty rough even if we could get through.

I said, "Let's go. If you say you can make it, why, I believe you can."

They stop at Bellefonte, up in the Alleghany Mountains, for gas, and I suggested going that far and then we could see how it was. Now here is a thing about these pilots: They don't have to take off unless they want to. It's up to them—they are the last word. The company knows that if it's physically possible to go they will go, so they let them decide.

Well, Brownie studies her over a bit and says, "Let's try it."

In the meantime it's cloudy and rainy here in Cleveland. Rain is not so bad; it's how low the clouds are—"visibility," I think, is the term. Well, I crawled into my fancy suit, they wheeled the plane out and we waved 'em good-by and took off in the rain. Well, we didn't do so bad for about an hour, and then we run into nothing but clouds. He is evidently trying to get on top of them, but they go right on up where we naturally suppose clouds to go. Then he had no room under 'em, so he is just making up his mind to go through. You can't see 100 feet ahead.

I don't know what it's all about, but I know they can't last forever and I know he knows what he is doing. Now we begin to hit little clear places;

64

after a while we commence to see the ground. Say, she is rocking and bucking like a bronc. I ain't going to make very edifying reading, but I started in to report this trip AS IS. I just like to ruined some of Uncle Sam's best mail sacks that were packed in around and under me. If any of you receive air mail along about that time you may remember and verify this story. Wow, but I am sick!

But I want to tell you little Brownie brought her through to Bellefonte, an air station away up in the mountains. Now ordinarily one pilot goes all the way from Cleveland to New York. But he is only going as far as Bellefonte and then turn the same plane over to another pilot.

Well, when we get here, this other pilot knew it was so bad he wouldn't take a chance in another plane; he wanted his own. They are all alike, but naturally they all have their special planes they are used to, and I am glad to see him ask to have all the mail changed over into his own. It will not only help his presence of mind but extricate me from an embarrassing physical position.

This was Pilot Thomas Nelson.[8] It was drizzling rain and the worst part of the mountains were to be gone over. It's getting late in the evening but not dark yet; the clouds are low. This field is in a kind of a valley; you couldent see the tops of the mountains for the clouds.

Well, we got up among them. Mountains and clouds and peaks all looked alike. We had been going mebbe an hour, mebbe a little less. 'Course I dident know anything about it; we might have been headed for Claremore, Oklahoma, for all I knew. I knew we were turning and twisting around a good deal; you couldent see anything or tell anything up there. Then I noticed he dropped down into a valley, a kind of a long narrow valley, and he started circling it. I knew then that he was looking for a place to light. It was pretty hilly. There was lots of prosperous old farmhouses but very few fields of any length. Everything was cut up with fences.

Finally he circled one place three or four times very low and he was getting the exact lay of the ground. It was raining hard now and getting pretty late—almost dark. He finally made his decision, made his last circle and dropped low, just missed the top of one fence so he could light as soon after passing it as possible, and he set her down. It had been raining there days steady and the ground was very soft, which helped to slow him up. He had a big load too. Then the ground was kinder uphill. He made as fine a landing as you could make at Mitchel Field, and stopped her a few yards from a wire fence.

I was kinder disappointed it come down so nice. I was just sitting there looking at all that mail around me. If it had tipped over on its nose, I was just thinking what a lot of fun they would have had picking air-mail stamps out of me. The letters would have been imprinted all over me. They would have had to send me around to the various addresses and let the people read me.

I dident know exactly what was the matter. He said when we stopped that he dident know just where we were—that we were off our course—and it looked so bad up there that he was afraid risking going into the night, off the lighted course.

Now there is just an example of what I told you about these fellows—they know what to do, and they don't take any chances. Had he been on his course, he would perhaps have gone on. But off it and dark coming and no lights, he had my whole indorsement in landing, and while he hadent landed in New York, he had landed. I was just on the verge of getting sick again anyway.

Well, he started over toward the nearest farmhouse. But, Lord, he dident need to. Here come people that hadent ventured out in the rain in three days over into this field where we had landed. He was about thirty miles south of his course, not so far from—I think it was the town of Beaver Falls—not Beaver Falls, New York, but Pennsylvania.

The wheels were away down in the mud and he said he dident think he could take off and get out of there anyway, so he advised me if I was in a hurry to go to the nearest railroad and go on to New York.

Well, by this time the Pennsylvania farmers were just thick; they all was mighty pleasant and nice, and wanted to do anything they could. If it had been lots of farmers they would have wanted us to take the thing out of there and give 'em relief. One said he lived right near and would drive me about twenty-five miles to some junction not far from Harrisburg, where I could catch a through train that would take me direct to New York. There was railroads nearer, but not the main line.

I hated to leave this old Kid, he was just a young fellow. But he said he would get them to bring him a truck and take the mail in to the nearest station and send it on by train, then phone Bellefonte and they would come early in the morning and help him get out. With no load, he thought he could make it.

Well, the farmer had a nice closed car and the rain dident matter. The fancy flying suit of mine had kept me dry, and the rain had washed some of the odor from it. I went by his house and while he was getting ready to take me to town, I went back in the kitchen by the stove. They was just gettin' supper ready. It seemed like old times on an old ranch back in Oklahoma.

I never saw as many things cooking at once. Believe me, those people sure do live back there. It was an old brick farmhouse over 100 years old, and the barn older, he said, than that. Those things cooking did smell so good, but my eating was over for that trip. I could still feel that Aeroplane dropping out from under me.

On the way in I asked him all about how they farmed and what they raised and how much the land was worth, and then I asked him if there was any Pennsylvania Dutch around there; that I had always heard of them and wanted to see some. It would have been like him landing in Oklahoma accidentally and wanting to see some Indians. He said there was a few here—that all that was around that car was of that breed. I says, why, they looked all right, and they talked pretty good English—that is as well as I could judge.

He said, "I am one."

Well, here I was with a Pennsylvania Dutchman and dident know it. He told me the old-timers do talk their language yet. They are great people and I liked the way they lived. I want to stop in there and stay a while again some time when I am feeling better.

Well, we got to the station and a through train come along pretty soon and landed in New York around midnight. If all had gone well and we hadent run into this bad storm, I would have landed at the field in Jersey at 5:30 in the evening and been in New York in time for dinner and a show, having left Beverly Hills, California the morning before. I got to bed, had a good night's sleep, got up next morning and saw the men and 'tended to my business, called around to see some more friends, and in fact had more time on my hands than I knew what to do with. It was still raining that morning. I went down to catch the train to go over to Hadley Field; it's out from New Brunswick.

I want to tell you now it don't do you any good to fly to New York. After I finally got out to the field I found I dident lose any time by landing at Beaver Falls, Pennsylvania; in fact I was nearer New York than Hadley, or even Mitchel or Roosevelt Field.[9] There is twenty Golf courses nearer New York than any flying field they have and it takes less ground to land on than to make a golf course on, yet the biggest City in the World has no regular place to land. You lose more time getting into the city than you save by flying there.

Well, I got to the field and it was just like yesterday in Cleveland; the weather was very little different. The ceiling was low. It was time to go, but it dident look like there would be anything doing. The pilot that was scheduled to be first off was William C. Hopson, an ex-army flyer—in fact 90 per cent of these men are all Army men; the rest are Navy or Marine.[10] I hunted up Hopson—Hoppy, they call him—I hunted up Hoppy. He looked at the map, talked to the radio weather operator. Finally he said he thought it was clearing and that we would go. It was raining there; but what was happening there dident mean anything. It is what is happening yonder that you want to know about. Well, sir, do you know it commenced to clear, and you know how clear and pretty it can get after a storm.

67

Well, we dident have a bit of trouble or a bit of fog. We got into Bellefonte and gassed her up and right on out to Cleveland. He set her down there, and as we taxied up to where all the gang was that we had left there the day before, why, he started to speak when I interrupted him:

"You would have made better time if you hadent been bucking a head wind."

Sure enough that was what he was about to utter. So I told the flyers that I was going to keep on flying till my beard caught in the propeller, or find a pilot that dident have a head wind to buck. Boys, I am flying till I catch a tail wind. And when I do and the pilot admits it, I am hanging up the helmet.

Here is the other plane all warmed up for Chicago; the storm is over and everything is working on schedule. I draw the same boy going back that brought me over, and I wish I could think of his name—an excellent Pilot and fine chap. By the way, this Hopson that just brought me in has since then set one down on the railroad tracks without any serious mishaps. I tell you those Guys are there.

We are late on account of leaving New York late, and it's getting good and dark before we get near Chicago. Then the lights—Ah, say, fly over a Big City at night! Daytime is like slumming compared to seeing a big lighted City from the air at night. The hundreds of lighted rows of streets running evey direction. You could see the dark outline of the Lake and the thousands of Automobile headlights moving like bugs. You could tell the revolving Beacon lights that he was being guided by. The course from New York to Chicago has lights every ten miles, and the lights from them cross, so that the Pilots are always within sight of a light, barring Fog. The field was all lighted with a great big row of lights around the out edges, besides the floods and beacons on the Hangars and towers. What a kick coming down, knowing you had left New York less than seven hours ago! Lunch in New York and dinner in Chicago.

They are changing the mail in a hurry. It's about eight or 8:30. Back into the closed Plane, and there is no other Passenger. That means I can lay down and sleep all night. I spent too many years riding in a day coach not to know how to curl up on one seat and sleep better than in most beds. They got a lot of lunch there, but I am not going in so strong for food as on the way east. That storm yesterday kinder spoiled my appetite.

Now let me tell you about this sickness. The air is just the same as the ocean. I am making no alibi's for it. If it's rough, you are liable to feel your stomach rising and falling with the Plane. But if it's nice and smooth, there is not a chance in the world of being sick.

This line we have just left, going from New York to Chicago, has a very

68

remarkable record that will compare with the Boeing or Western Air. They have only had it a short time—in fact since May. They have flown over 1,000,000 miles and no injury to anyone. They also operate the line from Chicago, down through Kansas City, Wichita and to Dallas. Their planes fly 5000 miles every day. Get the record of some bunch of Automobiles that have to run altogether 5000 miles a day and you will find they have got more cemeteries than they have cars. You don't have to stop to figure out which is the safer. All you have to do is to compare the intelligence of the men that Pilot Planes with the intelligence of everybody that drives a car.

But let's get home. We are loitering too much on the way with statistics. I take my overcoat and make it my pillow, and I am asleep before Pilot Lee leaves the ground.[11] All I know is that when the Plane landed at Omaha a few hours later, they had to shake me to get me out to change Planes. I hadent known about Gas at Iowa City at all. I asked Lee what kind of a trip we had.

He said, "We had a head wind most all the way in."

I said, "The winds are all blowing east tonight; night before last they were all blowing west."

I asked the Pilot that had just come in from Omaha, which was the opposite direction from which we had come from, what kind of a trip he'd had.

"I had a head wind most of the way and about three-quarters the rest."

Well, let's get back and get some more sleeping done. All you do this time is to change your head to the other side of the plane, which lays you on a new side. It was as warm and nice in there. I dident have on my flying suit or my overcoat. They say we got Gas in North Platte, but I hope they will pardon me if I admit I dident see the town. I was so restful that I don't even know who piloted the Plane on that hop. I believe it was Allison again, and the fellow that I couldent think of his name from Cleveland was Knoop.[12]

They wake me to change in Cheyenne. It's just breaking day. It don't look like the same gayly lighted place of the night before last. I do, however, distinctly remember this Pilot saying that outside of a head wind we had had a very quiet trip.

I got company from here on. He is the Engineer that is sent out by the Company that makes the Engines. He keeps 'em in shape. He was an awful nice fellow, and not near as broad as the other fellow. I had had a whole night's sleep and it dident matter much. I was getting in shape to take on nourishment again, so as soon as the vacuum bottle had been passed I begin to look over Wyoming.

Our Pilot on this hop from Cheyenne to Salt Lake was Slim Lewis.[13] Slim is quite a hunter and he asked me if I liked to hunt. So it's just good daylight as we leave Cheyenne. We have been going for perhaps three-quarters of an hour when —— I hope the company don't reprimand Slim by me being so mouthy as to tell this, for I don't imagine it was what he was exactly supposed to do. But I felt the Plane swerve on a short bank and I looked out to see if by chance we had hit a detour, and Mr. Lewis had his left wing tip right on the tail of a Gray Wolf. He scratched that Wolf's back for him for about 100 yards and then swerved back on the straightaway. The country was so level we were flying very low all the time. All at once he makes another razee and this time it's a bunch of Antelope.

Some of them seem to know old Slim and know he won't bother 'em. They sure did look pretty. Well, next comes a Coyote. He run him ragged for a few seconds; then more Antelope—about six bands in all; then over Lakes that had ducks, which Slim informed us he was coming back to get on his days off.

He knew every old rancher across Wyoming. They would all be out waving at him. This mechanic talked a good deal about Engines. But no more than I did about Acting. Finally I told him I dident know a thing in the World about Engines, that if they stopped this Plane and raised up the Hood and a rabbit jumped out, I would just figure he belonged in there. Begin to strike some mighty pretty little Ranches in the valleys over toward the mountains back of Salt Lake. You could see the little Lighthouse keeper's house now that it was daylight—Just about big enough to keep some matches in. We swooped down through the mountain pass and over beautiful Salt Lake City again.

Here is another great thing about an Aeroplane. You go over a country going one way and come back the very same route, but the whole thing will look different to you. It's because you are seeing it from exactly the opposite angle, and you will swear that you dident come that way before.

Back to the last leg of the Journey—Salt Lake to Los Angeles. I draw Alva DeGarmo as Pilot, and a good one.[14] We are over an hour late, which started by not leaving New York sooner yesterday. Oh, yes, Slim had the Pilot's wail as we pulled in:

"I had a head wind; considering it, it wasent bad time."

I was beginning to lose hope of ever catching a tail wind. I forgot to tell you about the Fares. It's the same coming this way as the other—about $407 for the one way, making the entire trip from coast to coast and back $814. And it saves five nights and four days.

We havent been gone over thirty minutes out of Salt Lake when I am handed a note. Well, it seemed like old times, and it sure was welcome. Eastern Pilots don't do that, because Eastern people don't do it; it just sorter belongs out here, where the Pilots want to be friendly and sociable. The other Boys back there are just as nice, but they don't know how their people might take them suggesting what some point of interest is. But I believe it's a good thing for all Pilots to do. The business is new and let's get anything into it that will get all out of a trip there is in it. So a little Note writing in the East wouldent be amiss. "Do you like a closed Plane or open one like this? I like the air myself, but of course we all know that the closed ones are the coming thing."

Now, you see, we got a friendly start.

Here is another that makes me kinder have hopes for a minute; "Dust on the ground shows there is a head wind down there, but we will stay up high—we are not getting much of it. We are making very good time. We left Salt Lake over an hour late."

And get this one:

"We will pass Milford in a few minutes, 165 miles out from S. L. We have only been an hour and thirty minutes—not bad for the old boat."

Another reads:

"That train left Los Angeles last night at six and won't be to Salt Lake till tonight at six. We will meet Jimmy James in a little while. He left Los Angeles this morning and will be in Salt Lake at two this afternoon—some difference."

"Here comes Jimmy!"

Now he was the Pilot that had taken me up three days before. He met us and circled around and flew alongside. He had a passenger. Then Alva returned the complement and we turned and circled back his way alongside of him. At this same time there was a train right underneath us—the Limited from the East. I bet they thought these two Aeroplanes were trying to catch each other, away out in that Desert, when they saw us monkeying around with each other.

We waved Jimmy good-by and away he went, and we went back to overtake the train again. The train was just at the time passing an old wagon that some old mover was going from one part of the Country to the other in. It was covered.

Now I got pretty good hearing when the wind is blowing right. There was a bunch of fellows sitting out on the Observation, fanning themselves and wiping the cinders off their faces and ordering ice water to try to keep cool while they were crossing the desert. As they passed the old fellow in a Wagon, they all looked at him. One spoke. But they all had the same thought, even if he hadent spoke it for them:

"Well, that's a pretty tough way to travel. Just think how the old-timers had to get from one place to another, and to think that poor devil is doing it still."

"Well, it's his own fault. Why don't he sell that old outfit and get on a train? It's his own fault."

71

"Well, some people just don't take to progress even when it's brought right to em," said another of the group. "Just think that fellow mebbe left Salt Lake before we left New York City, and this is all the further he is."

Another spoke up: "Well, the only way you can account for it is that he just don't know any better. It's people like him that can't see things that's holding this country out here back. They need some Eastern Pep and life and Go-getem, and wake-up-and move-around spirit out here."

I was sorry I couldn't hear more, but we were passing so fast that's all I could grab. I think I will go down to the Depot tomorrow night when they get in and hear the rest of it, for it's that go-getem Eastern spirit that we need. Here's another note:

"See this valley on your left? This will all be under water when the Boulder Dam is built. Did you ever see the Dam site? It's only over there about 15 miles off our course. If you would like, we will go by. We are making good time and can spare the time."

I sure did nod yes. Well, sir, we flew right over where it is to be built, and when some old Senator and Congressman gets up and tells about how he visited the place and looked it all over, it's a lot of Apple sauce. There is no road in there. There is only two ways to see it— that's to come down the Colorado River in a boat and the other is to see it from a Plane; and none of them ever did either, so ask him how he saw it. It's a natural place for a Dam if there ever was one. We circle all around it half a dozen times, down in it, over it and through it; then head off for Las Vegas, which we reach in a few minutes. There was at one place where we could see four states—Arizona, California, Nevada and Utah—all at once.

We get our gas and are away on the home stretch, flying away along down below Barstow. I told Alva that Brisbane lived not far away over on our right. He had no more than read the note than we swerved over and he asked me if I would know the place. I told him I believed I would from the description that Brisbane had given me of it. Sure enough, we found it—a ranch in a lot of Alfalfa, near the Mohave River. We circled it a few times and then out for L. A. We went straight over the mountains instead of going around through Cajon Pass. As we passed over the mountains he sent this:

"Reminds me of when I was a Forest ranger in a Plane up in Washington and Oregon. I was three years with them."

Now that gives you an idea how well equipped these Pilots are. Three years flying over mountain tops, hunting fires, with no landing fields, ought to make a fair Pilot. His next note said:

"This is my 275th Trip on this run."

He flew low right over Mount Wilson and then he shut his engine off and nosed her down and we just took a long glide from clear across

72

Pasadena and to the field. He passed me a note saying we had been making fine time.

Well, here we are, landing right where we started from four days ago. We left Tuesday morning, and it's now Friday evening at 5:15 P.M. He says we are fifteen minutes ahead of time.

"We made up the hour we were late and fifteen minutes more, besides all the side trips we had. We averaged right at 130 miles an hour. We caught a tail wind."

I fell into his arms and wanted to kiss him. Just think, I had finally ridden with an Aviator that caught a tail wind! I said I was going to quit when that event happened, but I'm not. I am going to try and get another one. My wife was there to meet me. She had had a very narrow escape. An Iowan in a flivver hit 'em crosswise, but they got him shoved off before any serious damage had been done.

On my way home I happened to think of my friend that had been in such a hurry to get to New York he had left a day before me. I looked at his time-table. He was now between Cleveland and Buffalo, and would reach New York tomorrow morning at 9:30. We were two hours getting from the field home—fifteen miles. We bucked a head wind all the way.

Let Us Pray They Don't Find Out
What's the Matter with the Movies

I can't write about the movies for I don't know anything about them, and I don't think anybody else knows anything about them.

It's the only business in the world that nobody knows anything about. Being in them don't give any more of an inkling about them than being out of them.

They, just a few months ago in New York, had a convention to discuss ways and means of regulating them and fixing a few of the things that they thought was worrying the industry. Well, it didn't get anywhere for nobody knew what was worrying the industry.

Everybody knew what was worrying him personally, but there was no two things that was worrying the same person.

The exhibitor said he wanted better pictures for less money; the producer said he wanted better stories and better directors and better actors for less money.

The actor said: "You are not giving me a fair share of what I draw at the box office." Will Hays said: "They got to be cleaner."

The exhibitor says: "If you get them too clean nobody is interested in them."

The novelist says: "What's the use of selling them a story, they don't make the story they buy."

The Scenario Staff says: "It reads good but it won't photograph." The exchange salesmen say: "The exhibitors are a dumb lot, they don't know what their audiences do want."

The exhibitors say: "We may be dumb, but we know how to count up. Give us pictures where there is something to count up."

The so-called intellectual keeps saying: "Why don't they give us something worthwhile in the movies that we can think about."

New McClure's Magazine, September 1928

The regular movie fan says: "Give us something to see, never mind think about. If we wanted to think we wouldn't come in here."

The old married folks say: "Give us something besides all this love sick junk, and the fadeout behind a willow tree."

The young folks that pay the rent on these temples of uplift say: "Give us some love and romance; what do we care about these pictures with a lot of folks trying to show what they do in life. We will get old soon enough without having to see it now."

Wall Street says: "We want more interest on our money."

The producers say: "Look at the fun you are having by being in this business. Didn't we give you a pass through the studio, what do you want for your money?"

The actors that aren't working say: "They don't want actors any more, they only want types."

The actors that are working say: "Thank God they are beginning to realize it's us actors they want and not just somebody that looks like the part."

Everybody is trying to offer suggestions how to regulate the business and bring it down on a sane basis. They are not going to bring it back on a sane basis. It will keep right on going just like it is now. It was never meant to be sane. It grows and gets bigger in spite of every known handicap.

You can't get a picture so poor but there will be an audience growing up somewhere that will like it, and you can't get one so good but what they will be forty per cent of the people that see it that won't like it. If it wasn't that way everybody in the world would go to see one picture. So they better quit monkeying with the business and let it alone. It's odd now, but it's odd in all of us movie people's favor.

The exhibitor that says he isn't making as much money as he used to, means that he is not making as much as he did last year or the year before but he doesn't mean that he is not making as much as he was before he got into this business.

The producer who says things are getting tough in the picture business, you suggest to him to go back into his original line of business and he will punch you in the jaw.

And the same with the actor, or anyone connected with the business, and the same also with the audience. He starts beefing about poor pictures, when he was never able to go before and get as much amusement for twenty, thirty, forty or fifty cents. He can't go into any other amusement business and better himself. If he could he would do it. He is doing better than he ever was in his life before.

He used to have to go to the gallery and sit in peanut hulls up to his chin, and come down a long stairs into a dark alley after the show, for more money than he can sit in a wonderful upholstered seat that he didn't even know existed till the movie man built his theater.

It's breaking pretty soft for audiences the same as for movie actors and producers and exhibitors.

Then the highbrow that says pictures are the bunk, let him try and find something that will beat them for twenty-five cents. There is no other branch of amusement in the world that has been brought right to his own little town, or if in a city, to his nearest street corner.

They are not bringing opera to your door step, or spoken drama to your neighborhood. You have to go to the city to get them. So don't start yapping about pictures. There is no law in the world that makes you go to them. No sir, you go to them because there is nothing that has yet been invented that can compare with them for the money.

These fan magazines are always yowling about, "What's the matter with the movies?" Try and get any of these editors to go back into their old newspaper work at their old salaries.

No sir, the movie business is a "cuckoo" business made by "cuckoo" people for "cuckoo" audiences, and as about eighty per cent of the world is "cuckoo" anyway they fill a spot that nothing will ever replace unless somebody invents something more "cuckoo."

Everybody is trying to find out what's the matter with them. If they ever do find out they will ruin their own business.

The movies have only one thing that may ever dent them in any way, and that is when the people in them, or the people going to them, ever start taking them seriously. That was one wonderful thing about dear Marcus Loew.[1] He made more money out of them than anybody, and he had the greatest sense of humor of any producer of them. But he always said, "I don't know what they are all about, and the more I learn about them, the less I know."

So go ahead, work hard, and do the best you can, but don't try to hold a clinic over the body.

Call them "arts and sciences" but do so with your tongue in your cheek. Everything that makes money and gives pleasure is not art. If it was, bootlegging would be the highest form of artistic endeavor.

So let's everybody connected with them, and everybody that loves to go see them, as we go to our beds at night, pray to our Supreme Being, that he don't allow it to be found out what is the matter with the movies, for if he ever does, we will all be out of a job.

There is Life in the Old Gal Yet, Al

Dear Al: I just thought I would take my pen in hand and drop you a few lines. This is not one of those "Too bad, old boy, we will get 'em the next time" letters. This is from an old friend who ever once in a while drops you a line, and tries to be truthful and lay some facts before you as they are, and Not as Political Leaders tell you they are.

Now, I knew you was pretty busy up to around November, and I dident want to bother you, cause this thing of running for President takes up just as much time on the Democratic side as it would on some side where you had a chance. Now you got time to sit down and think it over, I want to run over some things with you—talk over what we might 'a' done, pass over what we did do, and hold a sort of a Clinic over the old Democratic body and see just how much life there is in the old Gal yet.

Now let's get back and start at the beginning of this Presidential Bee that originally backed up to you and sit down. It was way back in 1920 in Frisco, when the Democrats had met to draft a Victim, and Franklin Roosevelt—who, with yourself, constitute just about the only two that anybody can pick for an All-American Democratic Team—he was just starting in on his nominating career of you for President; that was his maiden nominating speech.[1] He dident have it memorized then, and had to read it. Now, here is something that I want to bring up: If you remember, there was some talk of nominating Hoover at that same convention.[2] He hadent been back from Europe long and nobody knew just what he was. Some of 'em thought, on account of his working over there in such harmony with President Wilson, that he was a Democrat. Well, if they had known anything, that very fact should have showed 'em he was not a Democrat.

Consistent in Bad Luck

He had just made a marvelous record of full feeding some Belgiums, and he looked like a man that, on account of his uncanny ability of

Saturday Evening Post, January 19, 1929

providing food where it was impossible to get any, why, the Democrats figured that "here is the man that can provide nourishment for the next four years for us." Any man that can find grub for a Belgian in a war-strewn land, ought to be able to give political sustenance to a Party that looks like it will have the Post Offices shot from under them on November 2, 1920.

Now, while this fellow Hoover had been keeping our sugar down to one lump a day, and had us eating Bran—like a cow—instead of bread—why, if we had stayed on that bran mash for another year we would have sprouted horns—he had been slipping these extra Titbits which he was depriving us of, off to the gaunt and lean Armenians. But after his return over here he had enough spare time to detect that one of the Issues of the coming November Follies would be the League of Nations. Now, in his rambles all over the uncivilized World with his forked switch, which would turn down when it got over a certain piece of ground that needed some engineering feat to make it bear forth pay dirt, he had also stopped long enough to give Human Nature, as well as old Mother Earth's formation, a little study. In other words, his mind was not entirely on his trypod.

After his return over here, he had set up his sextant to get some observations on National Thought. He hadent peeped through the little mechanical gadget long before he discovered that this "pure and holy love" between Europe and ourselves was kinder listed to about forty-five degrees, on both sides of the water. His practical engineering mind showed him that we figured about as follows: We dragged Europe out of a Bog Hole once, but we don't want to have to stand there on the bank the rest of our lives to see if they crawl back in again. We dident mind feeding 'em, but we just dident wish to sign a contract with 'em. We might come over again if we wanted to, but we dident want to have any signed papers to that effect. Who they fought from now on would be their own business; if they over-matched themselves they would have to look out. In other words, we dident mind associating with 'em in a casual way, but we just dident want to get married to 'em.

Now, knowing these facts as he did, and knowing that the League of Nations would be the issue, he also knew that one Political Party would take one side, and the other the other. Now, although he had spent a great part of his life in Siberia and Patagonia, he had kept in close enough touch with American elections to know that in any question that had two sides—and if one side had a lot more people for it than the other—that a Party called the Democrats would pick the side with the fewest votes. Now, he knew that—and even the Siberians and Patagonians knew it. I don't know why it is, Al, but us Democrats just seem to have an uncanny premonition of sizing up a question and guessing

78

wrong on it. It almost makes you think sometimes it is done purposely. You can't make outsiders believe it's not done purposely. For they don't think people could purposely make that many mistakes accidentally. And what makes it funny is we get the first pick. It was practically the Democrats' war; their Administration had carried it through to a successful conclusion, and did a mighty good job of it, and naturally had the first guess as to what most of the people wanted to do after it was all over—did the people want to sign up with Europe or not? Now, it's as I say—the Democrats had their pick; they could have said, "No, people don't want the League." But they said, "Yes, we must have the League." See, they had the first pick and grabbed the wrong side by seven million. Now, Mr. Hoover knew that the Democrats would grab off the minority side, so he pulls his first wise Political move. He dident exactly say that he wasent one of you, but he dident allow you to use his name at the head of your Stationary that year as a Candidate for the Presidency. I really believe, if us Democrats had had anything good in the way of a Vehicle to get somewhere in, that he would have signed up with us. He seemed to have an open mind, but we just dident have any attractive proposition to offer him. If we had been smart, we would have picked him up then and said to him, "Here, write yourself out a Platform; we will turn the whole idea over to you, and all we want is results. We will even forgive you if you Don't mention "Jeffersonian Principles" and "Back to Jacksonian Democracy." All we want out of this thing is to be able to keep on handing out the mail." But no, we couldent see a Big man when he stood right before us. If we had turned our business over to him then, let him do the guessing on what side of a public question to get on, instead of us, we would 'a' been the side that would have got credit for all that Prosperity when everything was so high after the war.

Cold Business and Ideals

All you would 'a' had to do was to just get in and let the Government run itself. We had everything to sell after the war; the world had to buy it. Why, I myself could have taken the Government and Mellon, and made money with it. Then we would have been known as the Prosperity Party. So you see just how a few little wrong moves away back early in the game changes the whole destiny of Parties. If we dident know which side of a problem to get on, why dident we ask the Literary Digest to hold a Poll and find out for us? But No! We had Our Principles, Our Ideals! So we just lost the Post Offices for what looks like the rest of our natural lives. That's why the Republicans always get some where—They have No Ideals; It's just Cold Business with those Babies. You don't hear those Guys shouting about, "Get us back to the Lincolnian Principles, or the Taftonian methods." No, Sir, they know this is a fast-moving Country, that the people don't want to "go back" to anything; they want to go forward—or what they think is forward; it may be backward, but if they think it's forward, let 'em have their own way about it. But now to get back to my story: We let Hoover go, and he goes right over and signs up with the opposition as Secretary of Commerce as soon as the election is over. 'Course, it was not much of a job and not much of a Salary, but he showed that he was willing to start at the bottom if he could get in with some going concern. It was really no more than an Auditor's job. All he had to do was too keep track of how much we was buying and how much we was peddling to other Countries. They allowed him to come in and sit with the Cabinet, and several others was there in about the same capacity; and each one read their little reports—Hoover on "Exports— One Billion; Imports, Known—One-Half Billion; Imports, unknown— Four Billion." Then he was through for the day.

Then Will Hayes would get up and read his: "So many letters sent; so many letters lost; letters received, so-and-so." Then the Secretary of Agriculture would read his little say: "Farms in U. S., Eleven million; Farms mortgaged, Eleven million; farms carrying second mortgage, 10,998,634. The Department reports progress."

Then the Secretary of War would read his Department's record for the last week: "Wars, none; Peace, none; average, 50 per cent." Secretary of the Navy's Cabinet report for the week: "Ships, 950; ships sunk in compliance with Washington Disarmament agreement, 345. Would have sunk more, but run out of ammunition—some were very hard to sink. Cost of sinking, exceeded cost of building; would recommend in next Disarmament Conference that other Nations be asked to bear part of our sinking cost; also have learned from reliable sources—Not Diplomatic— that England and Japan, in accordance with our Disarmament Treaty with them, completed 83 Battleships each. The 5-5-3 Treaty is being strictly adhered to; we sink five in the morning, five in the afternoon, and they build three at night. I am able to report to the President and the Cabinet that on strict investigation I have found we can hold one more Naval Disarmament Conference, but not more. If we held a second one we would have to borrow a boat to go to it."

Jim Davis, Sec. of Labor, responded to the Toastmaster as follows: "Number of people laboring—ten million; people living off people labor- ing—ninety-eight million—including twenty-three million Government and State Employees.[3] Unemployment is confined practically to College Graduates and Harvard men. No prospect of relief for this type of unemployment untill education system is changed to teach them to work, instead of teaching them that with an education they won't have too."

Taking a Little Job Seriously

The Secretary of Interior arose. "On account of some slight Publicity having been attached to some previous leases made by Our Department, we can report nothing but Investigations during the past week." Attorney General responds to the toast: "What's wrong with Justice?" "I won't commit myself. If I did, I would be overruled by four of the Supreme Court, and the other three would vote, as usual, against the four." 'Course, then, that left no one there to talk over affairs of importance, but Sec. of State Hughes, Mr. Mellon, and President Coolidge; Dawes having in the meantime walked out on 'em, saying, as he fondled his old Possum-Bellied pipe: "Hell and Maria, these Cabinet wakes are dryer than a farm-relief Bill."

But this feller Hoover, instead of going out, like the other Cabinet Members, to play Golf when they finished reading their weekly reports, he used to kinder hang around to see what Calvin and Andy and Charley was gabbing about. They dident mind him, and he dident have much to say: In other words, he sorter seemed to take this Cabinet job kinder serious. He kept monkeying around with this Commerce outfit till he got it to amounting to something among Government Departments. So to humor and encourage him, they used to let him stay in the Cabinet meetings after all the others had gone, and listen to what Coolidge, Hughes and Mellon was discussing. He come in mighty handy if they had just got a Note from some foreign Country; he could tell 'em who, and where, the Country was. He knew most of the men personally that they were hearing from Diplomatically. 'Course, if it was from some Republican up in Massachusetts—in the old days, when they had Republicans up there—why, Mr. Coolidge would know who it was from; Hughes would know him if he had ever had a Lawsuit; and Mellon could tell you his Bank rating and all about his politics if he come from Pennsylvania—outside Philadelphia.

Knowing When to Refuse

Then, Hoover, being a great Red Cross man, he picked up a few Tornadoes and Hurricanes to kinder help fill in his spare time, and now and agin a flood to sorter keep his hand in feeding the destitute. The first thing you know he had made himself so valuable at it that it looked like we couldent have Calamity till he could get there to handle it. A lot of Calamitys that would have happened, we had to hold 'em off just on that account, for the man was booked up.

Then comes the Conventions of the summer of 1924. We better just skip over ours in Madison Square Garden. By the way, that was the only Calamity that Hoover was not put in charge of. He could have done a great relief work there, for there is nothing that ever come under my

81

observations that needed real Humane treatment worse than a Destitute Deligate. So we will get on to the Republican Convention in Cleveland— and there is where Hoover really showed himself a Genius. They wanted him to run for Vice President, and he turned it down; he knew what splendid care Mr. Coolidge took of himself. You see, he dident just grab at the first thing come along. He had an idea in his head, and was willing to wait for it.

What I am a getting at, Al, is this: This fellow is where he is today because he knew when to refuse something that he knew wouldent get him anywhere. He struggled along for eight years just practically as a Bill of Laden Clerk and a First-Aid Kit to Catastrophes, but look where he wound up. You see, all this is right along the line that I wrote you that other letter away back in October, 1927. I was trying to tell you, you got to wait for things till they are ripe; don't just jump into things, just because somebody offers it to you. Look and see if it's going to lead you anywhere. Now, after I wrote you that letter, a lot of your own Party thought I was all wet and dident know anything about it. Now I am not rewriting you any of that letter to rub it in, for you took your defeat in too good a manner. You was a good Sport and dident let out a single Squawk. But I repeat these to try and show not only you but the Party, why do we keep on doing things, elections after elections, that we absolutely know won't get us anywhere.

Here it is word for word, written a year and a half ago:

I, Al Smith, of my own free will and accord, do this day relinquish any claim or promise that I might have of any support or Deligates at the next Democratic Convention. I don't want to hinder what little harmony there is left in the party; I not only do not choose to run, but I refuse to run. But will give all my time and talents to work faithfully for whoever is nominated by the party.

And the following is the reason I gave you:

"Now, Al, if you will send 'em this letter you will look like you are sacrificing yourself, and in '32 they will nominate you by radio; they can't help it, and you will have a united Party. A half-wit knew you all couldent win in '24. Well, it's the same this year; you couldent put on a revival of Thomas Jefferson and get away with it.

"Even if they don't run Coolidge, they will let it be known that his same Cabinet will be retained. It's that Cabinet you can't beat, Al. But they can't stay in there for ever, and Prohibition, at the present rate of enforcement, will be much more of an Issue than it is this time. Let 'em nominate a Dry Democrat. Naturally he will be defeated, not because he is a dry but because he is a Democrat. Then, that will make your policy twice as strong four years from now. Al, don't let those New Yorkers kid you—this country is dry. Listen: If you think this Country ain't wet, you watch 'em drink; and If you think this Country ain't Dry, you watch 'em vote. When they vote, it's counted; but when they drink, it ain't. If you could register the Voter's breath instead of his ballot, it would be different. Besides, you got no Platform, you got no Issue, you can't ask people to throw somebody out just because somebody else wants in. You meet too many Democratic Leaders—that's what's the matter with the Party— these same Leaders not knowing any more about Public Opinion than they do. That's why they are Democratic Leaders."

Not Enough Votes Per Voter

"Then, you New Yorkers get a wrong prospectus of things. The outsider don't care nothing about New York, and if you think Tammany Hall is an asset, you just run and try to carry them with you, and you will find you have been overhandicapped. Now it ain't that you ain't strong, Al; you are strong—you are the strongest thing the Democrats have had in years. No Democrat could come near you—But it's not a Democrat that you meet in the finals; It's a Republican. Everybody is always asking, 'What's the matter with the Democratic Party?' There ain't nothing wrong with it; it's a Dandy old Party. The only thing wrong with it is the law killed it. It won't let a man vote but once, and there just ain't enough voters at one vote each to get it anywhere. You can't lick this Prosperity thing; even the fellow that hasent got any is all excited over the idea. You Politicians have got to look further ahead; you always got a Putter in your hands, when you ought to have a Driver. Now, Al, I am trying to tell you how to be President, Not how to be a Candidate."

But it's all over, and you made a great race—about six million votes better than anyone else in your Party could have done. And you give the Republicans the Durndest scare they had in years. You Had Mr. Hughes running around speaking every night, and any time anything can keep him up after nine o'clock it is a triple threat. And you got nothing to ever feel downhearted over.

Come and Bring Your Friends

Now, Al, I like you Democrats; you are sorter my kind of people, but I am just sick and tired seeing the whole thing mismanaged. So I have decided to take it over and see what we can salvage out of it. But you all got to take my advice from now on. If I see fit not to start an Entry in '32, why we won't start any. I am tired seeing good men killed off for nothing; I am tired seeing one Party that is not One Bit better than the other, Just Continually outsmart us. Those Guys can be beat, but Not with Jeffersonian and Jacksonian speeches. If a national question comes up, there is no sensible reason why we shouldent be on the Popular side, instead of the Right side all the time. Leave our old Political Leaders in the Senate, where they can't do anybody any good or harm, but hide 'em when a

Campaign is on; they been making the same speeches since they was weaned. There is absolutely millions of people in this country who are not even half pleased with the way these Republicans run things, but they prefer 'em to the Democrats' old-fashioned ideas. Now, taken out from under the influence of a lot of these old Mossbacks, you are a pretty progressive fellow, Al, and with you and this fellow Roosevelt as a kind of neclus, I think we can, with a lot of help from some Progressive young Democratic governors and senators and congressmen, why, we can make this thing into a Party, instead of a Memory. Get Raskob back on those Chervolets again.[4] He may know what Wall Street is going to do, but none of those Guys have got a vote. We don't need a Financier; we need a Magician. And let Norris and Blaine and the rest of them go back to where they come from—whereever that was.[5] That is one of the strictest rules I will have in the future: "Don't let anybody join us unless he is bringing somebody with him."

Now, I will see you around New York during the winter—unless you run onto something. I will write you more about my plans soon. They are all practical; they are not New, but they are new to the Democrats. With four years to work on, we may land Coolidge. Things won't look so rosy when he has to look at them from the outside.

Well, I must close, Al. Good luck to you and all the Smith tribe. Met your Daughter the other night at a dinner over at Mrs. Chas. Dana Gibson's.[6] Now, Al, while you ain't doing nothing will you do me a favor and work on that pronunciation of "Radio."   Yours,

WILL.

P. S.: Al, I am going to run this thing like Mussolini—that's what these Democrats need. I will even give 'em Castor oil.

84

Mr. Toastmaster and Democrats

MR. TOASTMASTER AND DEMOCRATS: I want to thank the previous Speakers, before they get out of here, for what they said about me. There is a few peculiarities that apply to the Democrat that don't apply to any other sex. One is, they will always leave as soon as they are through listening to themselves, and the other is they won't come unless they can speak. So I will direct my remarks to the rest of the audience that are left in the hall waiting to speak, and to the unseen Radio—that pronunciations is correct—audience who we, fortunately, can't see at this moment. We have no personal desire to know "How the other half lives." We are here gathered in festive array at Chili Joe's Greasy Spoon, celebrating my appointment as Manager and Supervising Director of the great old Democratic Party. In taking over this position I feel that I am replacing no one, or knocking anyone out of work; as it has been years since there has been either head or tail to the party. Now I am not doing this entirely out of the goodness of my heart. I have various reasons; among them is Sportsmanship. I think one of the greatest causes for the early hold that Politics had on our primitive Fathers and Grandfathers was the fact that it was a real race every four years, and they wagered money back and forth on it. There was even times in its early career that its affairs were so well managed that even-money betting was not uncommon. So it's my ambition and dream to try and return elections to that great speculative stage. As it's been run in latter years, it's a good deal of the same nature as the Stock Market. Betting on the Republicans has been like being a Broker—you couldn't possibly lose. Now that is what the economist will tell you, "is not a healthy condition." There must be some semblance of equality, or where does our whole structure of Government go? Why should the World's Series, Why should the Prize fight, Why should the misguided Greyhound persuing a Rabbitt that was sired by Edison, and who's Dam had a One-track mind—why should those things dwarf in speculative value the great National game of "Post Office; Who's got the Post Offices?" No, Sir, I want to see elections brought back to the good

---

Saturday Evening Post, March 30, 1929

Will Rogers and Mr. and Mrs. Babe Ruth at a Boston hospital in April of 1929.

old days, when a man would not only argue with you that you was voting for the wrong man but he would put up what should be the legitimate end of any argument, and that was the old Do, Re, Me. Back your judgment with Bat Hides—that's what you had to do in those days. And that's one of the main reasons I am taking over the Stage Management of this troop. I want to see elections made a gamble, and not a ratification.

Now, in order to not be misunderstood in this matter, I am taking the whole thing over, and relinquish all salary. I don't want a cent for the handling of the whole thing. I am taking it on a Commission basis. If I don't take the Party and make something out of it, I don't get anything. I know that that is very unusual; it has never been done in Politics before. Everybody always had some kind of a guaranty, but I am willing to gamble. I may be like an old-time Miner that has nothing to back up his claims but optimism, but I believe that we can take the old thing, work on her a good while, and make it go.

Not on account of any Traditions. I would have rather had the thing without tradition. That thing, Tradition, has held more things back in this world than a Red Traffic light. That's what hurts Harvard and Yale and Princeton; they are always having the Old Tradition drilled into 'em, instead of some forward passes. In the old days those colleges looked good because they didn't have to play nobody but each other, and thinking what their Forefathers did handicapped one of them as bad as it did the other; but when they commenced having to meet colleges that didn't know whether they had a Forefather, and cared less, why, that marked the decline of Tradition. Now I don't know what the Tradition of the Old Democratic Party is. I have heard of it all my life; for I was raised in what was sorter referred to as a Democratic atmosphere. It was in the Indian Territory, where we wasn't allowed to vote. That was principally on account of being Democratic that we was not allowed. In those days we had nothing but happiness to accompany the eating. We were Cherokees, or whatever your Indian ancestry might be.

New Schemes to Buy Votes

Then the Whites got to sneaking in from the North in such numbers that it looked like, if we got Statehood and a vote, that the thing would go Republican; so we got it, and it was our biggest blow to Liberty and Justice that we had ever received. Well, as a young Boy I didn't know a Republican from a Democrat, only in one way: If some man or bunch of men rode up to the ranch to eat or stay all night, and my Father set me to watching 'em all the time they was there—what they did and what they carried off—why, I learned in after years that they was Republicans; and the ones I didn't spy on—why, they were Democrats. For Democrats were loyal that way—they never took from each other. You see, we was on the lower side of the Montgomery Ward line during the Civil War between the Democrats and Republicans. And them Yankees from up in Kansas, such as William Randolph White, Senator Capper—who was even then relieving the Farmers of Kansas—and William Allen, and all of that Gang—we were the first ones to begin to doubt 'em.[1] You see, we was Democrats, but we wasn't allowed to work at it. And even then I used to hear 'em talk about Our Glorious Tradition, but the Speaker would never explain what it was, and even the ones today never tell you what it is. "Jeffersonian Principles" has always been a big sales argument with us Democrats. It seems that Jefferson was for the poor; well, that strikes me as being mighty good politics in those days; for that's about all there was. Nowadays, with everybody rich—or at least not wanting to be considered poor—now it would be political suicide to take the side of the poor. Coolidge solved it better than anybody when he said, "I am for Capital, but Not against labor." In other words, I love carrots, but I am equally fond of Spinach. Now, take the Jacksonian Democracy that has been used by more Democratic Orators than a bad cold has been used for an excuse to take a drink. The Jacksonian Democracy consisted of inventing the plan of giving everybody jobs according to how many votes they delivered to Jackson. "If he ain't of your Party, give him nothing. Charity begins at the polls." Then he would go back home, if he had happened to have been defeated, and pounce on the Indians and take it out on them. An Indian had no more right to live, according to old Andrew, than a Republican to hold a job during a Democratic Administration. So, as I say, that's about all I have ever been able to find out about our Traditional principles. So we are not going to do much along the Tradition line under my Czarship. It just looks to me like Democratic Tradition has about consisted of Running Second. We have spilled more oratory and convinced less voters than any party I know of, outside the Socialists.

Tradition is nothing more than saying, "The good old days," and what you mean by anybody's "good old days," is days they can remember when they was having more fun than they are now. So you can no more bring back your Tradition than you can "those good old days"; for no two things ever happen the same way twice. So never mind what has happened; we got to get out and figure "what's going to happen"; not only figure on it but buy enough votes so it's got to happen. I don't mean to buy all of 'em with money. We will just buy what we can afford to that way, but Buy 'em some other way—with facts, with Issues, with new schemes. No voter in the World ever voted for nothing; in some way he has been convinced that he is to get something for that vote. His vote is all that our Constitution gives him, and it goes to the highest bidder. He jumps the way his Bread looks like it's buttered the thickest. So what I am going to do is to figure out a sales Campaign that will prove to him that we can offer him more butter than the Republicans. Just look at this, for instance: The Republicans have run the Government and made money out of it for themselves. Now what we got to do is to show the people that we can run it cheaper for them. In other words, we got to cut the Republicans' price. It's simply a mercantile business in a town— that's all the Government is. Now the Republicans are established, they got the main store there. We got to come in; open up, and show the people we can give 'em as good or better goods at lower prices. Now, we, in order to do that, might not make as much out of it for ourselves as they are making, AT FIRST, but we have all got to kinder sacrifice immediate profits to what we can get when we really get going good. You see, they are bound to have people in this town that, while they are buying from them now, and have been for years, yet they are not satisfied. They would go to somebody else quick if somebody else had something to offer them. But we can't come in and open up the Store with the same old goods we used to have when we used to run a little Store years ago. We can't sell 'em cotton stockings, button shoes, calico, Horseshoe Tobacco and snuff; we got to sell em scented Cigarettes now. There is not five homes in any town now with a place for a fellow to spit. So we either got to swallow our tobacco juice or change with the times. You can no more sell a man Jeffersonian Principles than you could sell him a Croquet Set. He don't know what they are. If it happened that many years ago, and you have to explain 'em, why, they couldn't 'a' been much good. A Jug of Apple Jack and a chaw of Tobacco don't interest him along the hospitality line now. What he wants is a couple of shots of Rye, a niblick and the address of a friend.

When the Last Election Was Won

Then your Women vote is a-coming in today. So can that old long-Underwear stuff and show em some Step-Ins that are prettier than the Republicans'. You think they are a-buying "Glorious Tradition" at the polls? No, Sir, they want to know what kind of a break they are going to get in Commerce and Industry. If they have to make the living for the family, they want to know what kind of inducement the Government is going to make to them for doing it. They are no smarter than their Mothers were, but they think they are. So what we got to do is to make 'em think we think they are. Somebody humorously told them that they "swung this last election," and they foolishly believed it. So that will just whet their appetite for the next one. But Lord, the last election was won six years before, when Coolidge Just Let Nature take its course.

The Nineteenth Amendment—I think that's the one that made

Women humans by Act of Congress; in fact all the Amendments from along about the second or third, could have still been unpassed and Hoover would have made the same trip to Nicaragua. Women, Liquor, Tammany Hall—all had their minor little contributing factors one way or another in the total, but the whole answer was: We just didn't have any Merchandise to offer the Boys that would make 'em come over on our side of the Street. Our Store was open, but we just didn't have any Sale advertised. Our Ads consisted of enumerating the poor quality of the goods of our opposition, but we wasn't offering any longer lipstick for the same money than they was.

For Louder and Funner Bridge Parties

Look what the Automobile Industry did. They took out some of the Cylinders and put in Vanity cases, Cigarette Lighters, soft cushions. Who cared whether the thing would run or not. With present traffic conditions, you sit in a car hours, where you don't really ride in it minutes. And that's about the way with a Political Party that's in power; they stand, month in and month out, where there is not days that they are moving. So what we want to do is take the old thing and Doll it up. Make it look attractive to Women, put some pretty upholstering in there and show em that it's the Party for The Home. Never mind the Monroe Doctrine; promise them "we will solve the Servant Problem." "No Servant can leave without taking it up with the League of Nations." Tell em we are the Party that will observe the Sanctity of the Home. If we discover a Husband that says he is going "away on Business," we will look into his business and see that he don't take in too many Side lines. In other words, we will let the Women write our Platform; that's one of the oldest forms of Political Witchcraft, is to let some Society or Organization dictate some Plank that is to go in the Platform. That's in trade for the votes of that Organization; then, in return, not only their Plank or anybody else's is ever even walked on, much less used. A Congressional Record, Dictionary and Political Platform is the three least-used things in existence today. Oh, Yes, Sleeve holders comes in there too. Let us promise the Women Cabinet positions in proportion to the number of votes they give us. Show 'em some bargains. Get 'em a lot of Clubs and Societies they can belong to—they love that. Even get 'em some Uniforms. You know, next to the Darkies there is no one loves to get on some kind of an official Uniform like a Woman does. Study 'em, see what they want, and promise it to 'em. Why should the Republicans be the ones that have a monopoly of lying to the Women?

But quit trying to win their votes on the Tariff. What do they know or care about the Tariff? Ninety-seven and a half per cent of not only the Women of the Country but the men don't know what it is. It ain't worth the Broadcasting tolls. You might as well try to sell a Woman a Petticoat as Tariff. Make ours the Up-to-Date Party. Let em know that the whole thing has not just been renovated, but it's been rebuilt. Make it look like it's kinder fashionable to belong to it. That's what will bring the trade. We are the biggest Apes, or imitators, in the World of somebody that's doing just a little better than we are. If we can get a couple of bell Mares started, the whole Cavyyard will follow. So we will grab off a couple of Social Lions and Subsidize 'em, and we can land the Women like Mr. Coolidge shooting Turkeys. Never mind offering the Farmer something; offer the Bridge Player something. Also advertise: "Join the Democrats and stay out of the Bunkers." Don't drag in the howl about "The old Dinner Pail." Nobody has eat out of a Bucket since Big Bill Thompson fell out with King George. Drug Stores retail more meat than a Butcher shop does.

So what we will do is advertise a Sale, give em a bargain. You see, the trouble with the Democrats has been up to now that they have been giving the people "What they thought they ought to have," instead of "what they wanted."

Now I don't say for sure that I will start a Candidate in 1932; it all depends. If I am going to coach this lay-out, why, I will go into a Huddle with myself along in the summer of '32, and see what's doing. If there is rust in the wheat, Chinch Bugs in the Corn, Boll weevil thriving off the Cotton, Suckers slack in Wall Street, Price of Liquor less than cost of Production, Mellon declaring he is too old to serve again, Rockne leaving Notre Dame, Peggy Joyce settling down, Oklahoma impeachments at low ebb, Bad year for Babe Ruth, Dempsey refusing to come back that year—Let, as I say, all these above things happen in the spring and summer of 1932, and then I would get a training table ready and send in a Candidate.[2] Mind you, I wouldn't do it if all these had happened the year before or in 1931. You can have a Famine, Heel flies, and an Epidemic of the itch, all through the first three years of a Political reign, and then kinder pick up on the last year, and you can walk in. No voter can remember back a year. What happened in the last six months is as far as his mind can grasp. So that's why I couldn't possibly tell you in these next three years just what I will do; it all depends on that last summer. Napoleon said one time an Army traveled on its stomach— must 'a' had stomach trouble at Waterloo. Yet he was always noted more for his odd size than his apt remarks. Well, anyhow, I don't know what Soldiers do, but I know what voters do in regard to their stomachs. They go to the polls, and if it's full, they keep the Guy in that's already in, and if the old Stomach is empty, they vote to chuck him out. So, as Coach of the great Democratic Party, I am just going to sit and keep an eagle eye on the Stomach of the registered voter.

Watching How the Electorate Shapes Up

If I meet you and don't look you in the face, you will know why. Don't think it's because I don't want to recognize you; it's because I am watching your waist line. I will hold a Clinic over the not Body Politic but Body Human and see what's happening just south of the Diaphragm. In other words, along about June or July, 1932, I will put America to a tape-measure test, and if I find the center section NOT protruding, you will see a real Race in the coming November. But if I tap the public's stomach and it sounds like a Watermelon, we will just crawl back in with the Ground Hogs and won't come out as long as their middle makes a shadow. But the minute we see it receding toward the backbone, why we will pick up hope and be ready. In other words, you just can't beat a Party when the people are reducing PURPOSELY. But you let 'em start getting thin through lack of Nourishment and you can defeat the Party in power with nothing but a Congressman.

Then here is another thing that I have always claimed: You give the Country four more years of this Unparalleled Prosperity and they will be so tired of having everything they want that it will be a pleasure to get poor again. We are a great people to get tired of anything awful quick. We just jump from one extreme to another. We are much more apt to make a whole change than we ever are a partial change. If a Giant is all the rage this year, next year it won't be an ordinary-size man. No, we will jump right from the Giant to the Midget. I will watch that angle of our Sociology too. I may start a Candidate with the Slogan: "Come, Join the Democrats, and We will all be Poor and Happy and Moral again." You know, there is a lot of people getting awful tired of picking out every morning just what car to use that day. You work and skimp and make a million, and you find your next-door Neighbor just yesterday give away three million to build a separate Dormitory at some College for Cheer Leaders. Another acquaintance has given five million to get short skirts and bobbed hair on the downtrodden Armenians.

So I think the Republicans are over-doing this prosperity. You take our rich, now, on their vacations; they like to get away out and kinder rough it and pretend that they are poor again. They like to drive a little cheap make of car around personally. They just love to play poor, like a child loves to play dolls. You know, when you come home at night and find nothing in the Ice Box but Ice Cream and Cake, it finally gets on your nerves. When a stock market don't do nothing but go up, and all you have to do is Buy, why there is not much incentive for a man with sporting blood. Everything is going up because everything is amalgamating with something else. If you got a Business, and it ain't doing so good, why, combine it with another one and issue more stock. We are such

92

bargain hunters that if two things are put together we think they must be twice as good as they were singly. You can never have a failure in this Country as long as you can find something to combine with just before the blow-up comes. Why, they even nowadays combine things with no possible connection with each other. You just tie up with anything you can get to go in with you.

Where the Democrats Come In

It's an age of Big Business. I attended a Luncheon the other day where they were going to build the highest Church in the World. I suppose their Slogan will be, "Join our Church; we will guarantee to get you nearer to Heaven than our Competitors." They got to do these things; it's the Spirit of the times. But at the continual rate of combining, Democratic hope lays in the fact that everything in America will get to be one Company. It may be called the "Industrial, Agricultural, Spiritual and Recreational Company, Inc." It would embrace everything from Cigarette lighters to the Pennsylvania Railroad, from Vineyards to Wheat fields, from Alligator Pears to Brahman Heifers, from Golf Courses to Parchesi Boards, and would all be manufactured and sold by one big Corporation. Now, here is where us Democrats would come in. In doing away with thousands of these smaller Corporations that entered into this Gigantic Trust, there would naturally be millions and millions of Vice Presidents from these thousands of smaller Enterprises thrown on the mercy of the World. Now they are naturally not going to feel any too well toward this new order of Big Business; for there is nothing that a Vice President can do but be a Vice President. You take that title away from him and he can't hand you a Card. And you take away all the Vice Presidents' cards that are handed out in a year, and you have just left them destitute of employment. But they can still vote. Losing your Vice Presidency don't lose you your Citizenship. The founders of the Constitution was liberal in that respect. So that's where this tremendous combination of big business is eventually going to act against the Republican Party. Every combine throws these billions of Vice Presidents out of work; that means another dissatisfied man, and another dissatisfied man means a Democrat.

Dissatisfaction is what makes you a Democrat; it's not "environment" or "training" or "education." In fact, the more education he gets the less apt he is to be a Democrat, and if he is very highly educated he will see the Apple Sauce in both Parties. And training—you can't train a man to be a Democrat. He acts like he is trained, but he ain't; most of that devilment he just come by naturally. Environment don't either hurt him or help him.

He can run with a bunch of Republicans for a year and come out as honest as he went in, and he can run with a bunch of Democrats for a year and come out knowing just as little as he did when he went in. But dissatisfaction is his stock in trade. He knows the Republicans are Sharpers, but he don't know enough to prove it on 'em; and the Republicans know that they are Sharpers and know that the Democrat will never know enough to prove it on 'em.

The Same Old Corruption Plank

But give us the vote of all the Vice Presidents and we will drive these Republicans back to manual labor again. But I don't want to branch off speaking here tonight before this assemblage on Corruption. I certainly am not going to make that usual mistake that the Democrats make every time an election comes up. We have talked more Corruption and got less of it than any known denomination. Americans are funny people; they never get het up over anything unless they are participating in it. The fellow that ain't getting any Corruption, he don't think that it can possibly be so common, or it would have reached him, and the ones that are getting some of it don't want it brought up. Jimmy Cox run on Corruption in the Republican Party, and there was seven million more people in favor of it than there was of abolishing it. Mr. Davis resurrected the same platform in 1924, and eight million more were in favor of it—a clear gain of a million in four years that were living in hopes of getting their clutches on some of it. Instead of by this time having learned that it was an Asset in Politics, why, we Democrats dragged it out again in '28, and lost everything but Rhode Island and Arkansaw. You see, this Corruption thing really started with us Democrats. They used to always pick up a few dollars around election times from the Saloon Keepers. It was just a small petty graft. In fact, I think Tammany Hall kinder originated the idea—that was back in the old days, before the 1928 Restoration. Then the Republicans come along and saw what the Democrats were doing with just a few Saloon Keepers, and said, "Here; why won't this same thing work in a big way? Won't Lumber, Coal, Banks, Mines, Manufactures and big things donate to a fund, if we can kinder promise to give 'em some Tariff now and ag'in? Us being in office, we can kinder throw some little things their way, the same as the Ward Politician can keep opposition from opening across the Street from Murphy's Place." So they took it up. It was really an idea that had belonged to us, but they saw what was in it, and brought it up to the high plane it is today. Now, it was not exactly what the coarse would call "Corrupt"; it really come under the heading of Political Reciprocity. The Democratic Politician helped out the little Saloon Keeper, and the Republican Leader helped out the Banker and the Merchant. What I am trying to prove to you is that right from the jump these Republicans had

BIG ideas. Our side was great originators, but these Guys improved on 'em; they would make something worth while out of it. I hate to admit it, Boys, but those Birds are just shrewder than we are. We have always had our eyes on a Dime; they have always had theirs on a Dollar. That's why the Democrats can stay in Power in City and Town Governments, but when it comes to getting our fists into the National Treasury we are handcuffed. The Republicans won't monkey away their time with some little local City election. They know the Dough is on the Potomac, and not in some City Hall. We worry our heads off over "who is going to be Sheriff or Justice of the Peace," and their minds is on: "What two high-binders will we send to the Senate?"

Now, we are all here together at this dinner and there is no use kidding ourselves; we are just naturally the cheapest of Political Organizations. We are a happy lot, though; we are in just as good humor when out of Office as we are in. We are just like a Life Prisoner who has been made a Trusty; we know we ain't going to do anybody any harm, and they know we ain't going anywhere. We are just kinder tolerated for the laughs we hand out every four years.

The Great Revelation

There is one thing about a Democrat: He would rather make a Speech than a Dollar. In fact, that's our downfall. We start in with pretty good prospects, but we manage to talk ourselves out of enough votes by November to finish second. During the last election nobody will ever know the amount of votes lost by each of the candidates. We know the amount of votes that Radio cost the two collectively; for there was seventeen million more people registered that didn't vote at all. There was that many people that had originally made up their minds to go to the trouble of voting, but after they heard Both of them over the Radio, they didn't go at all. That would be just like a thousand people out of three thousand, after buying their Tickets to a Show and then hearing the first Act, walking out and not staying. Now, as I say, nobody knows which one was responsible for this falling off. It must have been both of them. They talk about what a great thing the Radio has been for Politicians and Candidates. Why, there has been more people got wise to over the Radio than Senate investigations have exposed. Nothing in the World exposes how Little you have to say as Radio. So that is one thing that we will save a lot of money on during any Campaign that I decide to enter a Candidate. When he is nominated we are going to have him say "YES," and if he says anything else from then to the first Tuesday after the first Monday of November of that year, we will swear that it was said by a Spokesman who was not Official. Mr. Coolidge didn't Come out on anything; yet he come out in better shape than any President that we have released in many years. His opinions on every Deuce or Tray that turned up during his Administration was not Blabbed over any organized Wave Length. He never expressed his opinion on a thing to a soul; only Laddie Boy, and Laddie Boy died with the secrets intact.[3]

A Real Public Benefaction

Now, the only way we ever learn anything is from somebody's past experience; so I am in the Market for a speechless Democrat. That is going to be harder to find than it will be to elect him, but we will sure keep him quiet during the Campaign. Now, I can't tell you now what the issues will be—that's too far off—but one thing I will assure you now: It won't be any of the ones that have been used these past years. What we want to do is to string along with these Republicans in the Senate or House, and when something accidentaly comes up that is good for the Country, why, put it over. In other words, get in there and act like you was working for the Taxpayer instead of exclusively for the Democratic Party. Vote "YES" on something besides widening the Chatahoochie. Cut out that balloting on things in private. If you haven't got the nerve to let the people know how you stand on anything, have a sick friend, and go home and sit up with him on the day of the vote. But try and be nonpartisan; you would be surprised how quick the people of all Political denominations will find it out. If the Senate wants to take a secret vote, let it be known that the Democrats were against it to a man. In other words, you got to shame the Republicans into decency. But in doing so you will make a rep for yourself. I wouldn't take a Party any longer to show that it was Progressive than it would an individual. Borah, just for Campaign purposes, was listed as a Republican. But look how quick he lived it down. Now, you would be surprised at the amount of people that think he is working for the people.

Now you are to come back soon and work on Farm Relief. If it looks like you can help the farmer, why, do it. Don't kill it off just because Hoover happened to be the one that had to try and look like he was doing something for 'em. Now I inherited a lot of you when I took over the Management of this Outfit, and there is a lot of you that won't be in my new Organization. You just don't fit in with my new scheme of things. It takes a long time to get anything through a Politician's mind. For instance, we elect in November, but don't seat till the following March—that was because in those days it took that long to get to Washington. Now we can't change it, because we just can't elect anybody that is Big enough to say: "They don't want me in here and I am willing to resign and let the new Congress in now." If all the Democrats would do that one session, and show that they was the BIG Party, and wasn't just looking to hang on—their Forefathers hung on because the other fellow was on his way from Oregon with a yoke of Oxen—why, that very thing would stamp 'em as real public benefactors. You are the only people in the world that wants to work on after you are fired— that's, of course, just one little thing, but it is doing dozens of little things like that, that will get people out of the habit of believing that, in case the Democrats get in, it will be a return to Slavery, Chain harness and Bustles.

The Hoofing Kid from Claremore

Ever since I been trying to write (to keep from manual labor) I always did want to write one of those "success" Articles. They have always appealed to me as being the most interesting reading, for we all want to know just how our rich and our well-known people got that way. But I just never could get near enough to anybody that had done anything out of the ordinary to get one of those Stories.

I would pick up this well-known Magazine and read how some fellow used to work in a store and he sold more things for ten cents and five cents than he did for any other amounts, so that gave him the idea of handling nothing but things that sold for five and ten cents. It told how he had worked hard, and took advantage of his oppurtunities, and when success came one night and knocked he already had the door open. Well, you know that made mighty good reading; it inspired the young to be on the lookout if they saw something coming down the road disguised as Oppurtunity.

I forgot to tell you this fellow that grabbed Old Man Oppurtunity by the nap of the neck and pulled him in dident turn out to be a soul but Woolworth.[1] Now he has a tower in New York where for twenty-five cents you can go and see what he done for a dime. Now, you see how those writers can take those happenings and make 'em so interesting. If I had reviewed his career, I would have just said, well, here is a Guy that was smart enough in his youth to see that just about everybody he come in contact with just had a nickle or a dime, and he said to himself, "That's the people I am going to string with till I get their dime."

Then I read where my good friend Charley Schwab just jumped from the Presidency of one corporation to another, and couldent seem to get settled, and he finally made him one of his own where he would be the President and the Board of Directors and everything—then he wouldent have any arguments with anyone but himself.[2] Oh, and just oodles of others that had made a success, I had read about in your magazine. Even Coolidge was in there. It told how he had started with practically no

American Magazine, April 1929

political job at all. But he worked hard to hold it, and finally a better one was offered and he was right there to take advantage of it, and he had just worked himself right up, and always for the same corporation, Politics all the time. He saw that Politics was going to amount to something some day so he persevered, and had a good job for nearly six years.

I wanted to just be one of these fellows that wrote about some man that had got somewhere by "hard work, perseverance, and taking advantage of his oppurtunities."

Well, the other day I am hopping from out around Hollywood, to get away from everybody practicing talking (trying to stay in the picture business). You know, everybody out there is walking around carrying a Dictionary, learning to pronounce words, and getting what they call their "Diction" working right.

But this is not about Beverley Hills or Hollywood. This is about Claremore, Oklahoma, a town that reached its enviable position through hard work, perseverance, and water that will cure you of everything but being a Democrat. Well, I dropped in there between gigles at something the Presidential Candidates had said seriously; I was just trying to keep my tongue in my cheek till election. So I do pop in unexpectedly on the old home and what do you think the old County seat town is doing? I see by the newspapers that they had given a big reception to their great runner, Andy Payne, right there in old Claremore, the home of Radium water, which would not only cure you of whatever you had but would enhance your sense of humor.[3] Why, we have had men that come there on a stretcher who had never laughed at a Ford Joke in their lives, and after ten baths, had left in a second-hand one just laughing themselves into an early accident.

The Chamber of Commerce for once had joined with the Lions, Tiger, Apes, Wildcats, Rotarys, Kiawanises, and the young Democrats in giving to Andy a reception befitting one of the old Greek Hoofers in Athens when he had run in 30 or 40 miles to tell them there was a Restaurant site open up around Thermopole. I felt kinder jealoes when I read that someone had supplanted me as the favorite son. Wasent I to Claremore what the Dairy Industry is to young Bob La Follette in Wisconsin?[4] Wasent I the local Borah? Where did Andy come to be running in grabbing my thunder?

Well, that afternoon I drove out to the farm in the Country where Andy lived. It was about 8 miles from my old ranch place where I was born and raised. Andy's Daddy, Doc Payne, he wasent a Doctor, he was just a cow-puncher there is his early days, and afterwards got him this farm.[5] Well, I was raised with Doc. He lived right near and used to work on our outfit and he and I pretty near learned to ride and work stock together. He is part Cherokee, and this Kid is part Injun.

When I read about some boy from Claremore leading the race across the whole United States I dident know it was Old Doc's boy. These Kids had all grown up since I left there. I wondered how it could be, for Doc couldent run across the barn lot. Well, I went out and had a great visit with 'em. I wanted to see this lad who had I think won the greatest endurance test that has ever been put on during our or anybody else's time.

Let's get down to what that thing was. It was a foot race from Los Angeles to New York—not direct, but around by any town that would dig up a few hundred dollars to get them to run through it. When they got to St. Louis they went up by Chicago, to get to New York. Now, if you made that roundabout trip on the train, R. R. officials would think you were cuckoo. When they got to Chicago if somebody had offered Pyle, the Manager, $5,000, he would have had them go by the way of St. Johns, Newfoundland.[6]

Some three hundred left Los Angeles, and I think about 50 finished. There was great Marathon runners from all over the world entered. The race was kidded all over the Country as the "Bunion Derby," just because it was a freak idea and was being done by this fellow Pyle, that the sporting Writers had always taken much pleasure in rawhiding. Had Tex Rickard put it on and the men run half as fast, and took twice as long, it would have gone down in Sporting annals as "the greatest test of stamina and grit that had ever been performed by man."[7]

But Pyle put it on, so it must be funny, or a fake. You can put on a prize fight or a Boxing match for one night and fake it. But no fake runs 86 days, with the most critical audience in the world watching them every day to see that they dident catch a ride, or cheat in some way. Think of that, a test of grit that lasts 86 days. Any other Athaletic event is over in a few minutes or an afternoon. But think of getting up every morning for 86 mornings straight without a day off and having to run from 25 (the shortest day) up to 80 miles. If you wasent in by a certain time (midnight that night) you was out of the race entirely. Your time was kept each day, you was checked in and out, every day was a race of its own.

A sporting writer will rave his head off over some football player making an 80-yard run. What would he do if he had to run 80 miles, and do it again the next day, sick, sore feet, bad colds, bum feed, cramps, blisters, no time to lay up and cure 'em, always had to get out in the morning, rain, snow, sleet, desert heat, always be there, ready to go? A Marathon that they train for years for is a little over 26 miles. Then they come in and faint, and crowds carry them off. You couldent faint in this race, nobody to carry you off. If you did, you just layed there, maby some car run over you, but that was about all you could expect.

Tunney, our Champion, would take a year and a half to get ready to fight 30 minutes, with a minute's rest between each three.[8] What would one of these foot racers thought of thirty minutes of physical work? They even write about a "hard Golf Game, that Stamina won out in the end." There is not a Golf Player that could have made this trip in a car without restoratives. Baseball players knock a three-bagger and have to sit on third base to rest till somebody knocks a home run to bring 'em in. Why, we havent got a sporting writer that could run a block to catch a street car every morning for a week without fainting. What I mean, they never did give the credit it deserved. Just because it wasent popularly managed.

But what did that have to do with what these poor fellows was going through with every day? If Coolidge and the Prince of Wales had managed it, that wouldent have made it any easier to run.[9] You had to do the stuff, no matter what kind of publicity it got. So that's what made me think that, Mr. Editor, it might fit in with your scheme of things. It looks like I had found a man that "worked hard, persevered, and took advantage of his oppurtunities," and that's what got him not only where he is today, but from Los Angeles to New York.

He was only 19 years old, he had never raced but very little, run for his little Country High School there at Foyil, but no long-distance races at all. He told me lots about the race. The hardest day was coming into Amarillo, Texas, through the mud; then it hailed on 'em. Willie Kohlemainen, the great Finn runner, started but he dident last till they got outside the Los Angeles City Limits.[10] (Which by the way is some race itself. You enter Los Angeles City Limits just a mile west of Phoenix, Arizona. Bakersfield is the northern boundry; they would have annexed Salt Lake but the state line stopped 'em.)

A Full-blooded Indian started.[11] But they put shoes on him and he couldent run; civilization was too much for him. Salo the Finn that finished second to Payne in New York, Andy thinks is a great runner, and a very fine, square chap.[12] He said they sent Policemen with him when they run into Passaic, on account of his being ahead of Salo. Some thought the people there might do something to put him out of the race. But he said he was never treated better than by the folks there, and Salo's own friends. This Gavussi the Englishman that was leading up to near Cleveland and dropped out, Andy thought he was a great runner.[13] A colored boy, Eddie Gardner, was doing fine but the Ethiopian hospitality along the road loaded him up with too much chicken and Dumplings, and water mellon.[14] He says, "I don't care where I finish, the Black folks will take care of me," and they did. He and Toby, a little "Jig" only 18

101

years old—the harlem black belt made them up a purse of over a thousand dollars.[15] Toby wanted to run back to see what the ones in Los Angeles would give him.

An old Whiskered Guy was with 'em. He claimed he had been in the Movies. He told along the road that he played Abraham in DeMille's version of the Bible, and that he was Moses in another one of Cecil's plays, by the same Author, Jeanie McPherson.[16] Well, he was getting over big with the ones who dident remember who Theadore Roberts was, and H. B. Warner.[17] Andy said this old Boy did kinder look like some of the pictures of some of the old diciples.

Well, Moses reached as far as Illinois somewhere and somebody spied about a yard of his whiskers sticking out of the tonneau of a charitable Lady's Sedan. He had forgot to tuck 'em all in on his run this day, so he was, as we say in Vaudeville, "Shut," or "Closed." They had suspicioned that he had done some automobiling before. But he had always nestled his spinach in with him, till this day. He claimed that it would be much against him in Pictures, when they found out that Moses had stolen a ride, but that was one of the strict rules, so Moses went back. When he got to the Mississippi it is not recorded if it opened up and let him through. But I guess he went home and shaved and is maby playing in "Our Gang Comedies," maby blacked up and is "Forena's" little brother.

They all told me out around home that the only reason Andy won the race was that his sister sixteen years old was not in. She is better than Andy.

I asked him how he did about his feet. I knew that in a long race like that, keeping their feet in good condition was the great worry. He said, "I dident have any trouble with 'em."

I then asked, "Well, what did you do to keep 'em in shape?"

"I dident do nothing. I just washed 'em every once in awhile."

Now, this old Oklahoma high-school boy outrun all the best runners in the World for an entire summer. He accomplished this by being "alert and taking advantage of his oppurtunities when it come along." But do you want to know the real reason he won? Well, they are one of the only families that dident own a automobile. He used to run to school. So the moral of this success story is, Dont own a car. If each one of our Athaletes in the races that went to the Olympics had never owned a car, we would have won every race there. Those Finns, like Nurmi, would just take an arm full of Herring and just trot along and look back at our Kids who had been used to riding around their College Campuses in an old flivver with a lot "wisecracks" on it.[18] The only way we will ever win another International foot race is send flivvers to Finland.

First and Only Presentation of a Humorous Sketch Entitled

"COOLIDGE"

Episodes by Dwight Morrow

Written and Produced by

Will Rogers

PRIVATE CITIZEN COOLIDGE has entered the writing field in direct and almost unbeatable competition with the rest of us real high-class Literary Lights, and he has us swamped. No one had any idea that he could write such human and plain, straightaway, interesting stuff. If he had ever made one of his speeches that interesting while he was in there, he would have been elected for life.

That kinder brings up the question: "Who writes these longwinded, uninteresting messages that our Public Men deliver?" It must be one man in Washington that turns 'em all out, for regardless of who is President they are the same ones, and different men couldent possibly think of the same things year after year. It's some guy down there who has the speech contract. You just call up and say, "I want an Acceptance speech," or "I want a Decoration Day speech; I want a Farm Relief speech; I want a Country is Doing Well speech; I want a Friendship for All Foreign Nations speech."

Well, whoever he is, he is not the one that suggested Lincoln's Gettysburg speech. But it looks like he has written all of 'em since then. Course, Presidents having that Senate on their minds all the time they are in there dont add any to their peace of mind, so they really are not themselves. But the minute Mr. Coolidge got out of there and dident have to be bothered with the Senate, why, he just up and makes himself even more human than any of us.

Now he is going to write a lot of those interesting things for this

American Magazine, June 1929

Magazine, and the Editor tells me they are great. Course, an Editor will say that to everybody but the one that is writing the stuff. They are afraid to brag on him—he might want more money—and I bet you Mr. Coolidge is getting wise quick, too. It certainly does seem awful appropriate that he should be writing for THE AMERICAN MAGAZINE. For it features human interest stories. Now he is going to tell you a lot about himself and his work, but there is going to be a lot of stuff that he wont tell you. Modesty alone would forbid him mentioning lots of the things that I am going to tell you, and no one has ever accused Mr. Coolidge of not being modest. I have had lots of dope on him for over a year, but him being President, why, naturally it wouldent seem very appropriate to use it then.

When you want to get a line on a fellow, dont get it from the man himself; get it from someone who knows him. Now, I was in Mexico about a year and a half ago, and I traveled around on the train with Ambassador Morrow and President Calles for a couple of weeks; then back and was at the Embassy for a couple more.[1] Mr. Morrow and me only had two topics of conversation, Coolidge and Calles. We were doping out what kind of a fellow Calles was, and I was trying to find out from Mr. Morrow if his friend Coolidge was going to run again. He had issued his famous "I dont choose," but I believed that he had spent many days with the Dictionary finding that exact word, for I had never heard of a word that more nearly meant "Yes, No, Maby, Cant tell yet, Perhaps, and Dont want to, but will in a pinch."[2] Morrow naturally thought that he meant it, but that there might be (what do you call 'em) extenuating circumstances. Now, we all consider that Morrow knows Coolidge better than anybody else (which dont mean anything), for Morrow would often remark, "I dont know him at all." But in sitting night after night arguing it out he naturally told me many things of Mr. Coolidge.

I am not going to try and tell 'em to you in a routing from the time that they entered Amherst, but just sorter like Mr. Morrow told 'em to me. The most impressive one, of course, to me was what he told Morrow after being sworn in as President. Morrow, of course, went down to Washington as soon after this event as possible to pay his respects and wish his old friend well. But let's just let Mr. Morrow testify in this case —"Coolidge vs. the People." Now, Mr. Morrow, you take the stand and tell what happened when you first saw Coolidge after his being made President, and any other things, no matter how small, or how insignificant, that might be relevant to finding out something about this rather silent man. Just tell it in your own way.

"Well," says Mr. Morrow, "I got down there and visited him at his Hotel, for he gave Mrs. Harding plenty of time to get her things out of the White House, for which she was always tremendously appreciative.[3] I was in the room with him for a long time and he dident say a word. That wasent anything new; I had seen that happen many times before. When finally he turned to me and said, 'Dwight, I am NOT going to make the mistake that lots of them have made; I am NOT going to try and be a GREAT President.'

"Now, that's all he said. But wasent that great? You know, Will, Coolidge is not awed by the importance of the Presidency. He has told me since that he just considered it a *Chore.* (You town boys wont know what a chore is. It's just one of the various evening jobs that must be done around a farm, like milking, chopping wood, and feeding stock.) You see, with every President the job has meant something; with Wilson it was his Dream, with Roosevelt it was a Lark, with Taft a Laugh, and with Harding a Nightmare.[4] But with Coolidge it was just a Chore—a thing he was going to go about in the ordinary routine of the evening's work. He dident enter it with any Great Ideas. Neither did he enter it with any Great Humility. He figured it's just one of the jobs that we have in this country to do, and he happened by chance to be the one called on to do it; and that's where his success has come from.

"I will never forget one time Mrs. Morrow and I were there. The Oil Scandal was at its heighth, and it looked like heavy things were brewing. Coolidge turned and looked out of a window, then said, 'They say that Lincoln could look out of that window and see a Rebel Flag flying. Well, I guess nobody since Lincoln has had that much to worry about.' Now, how you going to beat a fellow that keeps his feet on the ground that way?

"You know, he is quite a character, this fellow. We were dining at the White House one night. It was kind of a New England Boiled Dinner. Speaker of the House Gillett was there, he and his wife.[5] They were old family friends of the Coolidges. Well, dinner was served promptly at seven as usual. After dinner us menfolks retired to a room and smoked and chatted for fifteen minutes; then we joined the ladies. We were in there not over thirty minutes, which brought it up perhaps to 8:45 or 9 o'clock. He got up, shook hands with all of us, says 'Good night,' and was off to bed. We go down to get our cars at the door, and Gillett's driver was not there—he evidently had gone for his own dinner and hadent yet returned. Gillett turned to me and said, 'Dwight, I have been here for dinner a dozen times, and I order my car earlier every time, but I have never yet been able to order it early enough.'

"But, speaking of dinners, I must tell you about the first time we ever entertained the Coolidges when our children were present. It was at the Touraine Hotel, Boston. He had just been made Governor, and he and Mrs. Coolidge dined with us.[6] There were several in the party. My daughter Anne had her finger tied up from some little trivial accident.[7]

105

After the company had all gone, the girls were all remarking how quiet Gov. Coolidge was, that he hadent spoken to anybody hardly during the whole evening. Then Anne spoke up and said, 'Well, I like him; I think he is fine. He is the only one in the whole party all evening that noticed that my finger was hurt.' Now, of course that is just what he would do— he could do that without taking chance of being quoted on what he said. He would discuss sore fingers with you lots quicker than he would subjects of State.

"Did I tell you about the time when we were graduated from Amherst? Well, we had been pretty friendly during our course and one day I asked him, 'Calvin, where do you expect to set up in your law practice?' naturally figuring that he would try New York, or at least Boston, or Springfield. He said, 'I am going to stay here; I dont believe in going any further for anything than is necessary.' And he did stay there, right there in Northampton and became President. A lot of the rest of the class started running around to big cities, and now you cant find 'em. He stuck right where he come from and got elected to everything that has an election attached to it. He was Lieutenant Governor of Massachusetts and had one room at the old Adams House. He was elected Governor, and instead of taking a house, he just took another room (at a rate).

"He was in the Legislature away back in the early days and I went up to see him one time. (At that time they elected their Legislature every year.) He was also studying and trying to practice law. So I asked him, 'Calvin, how do you manage to work this? It must take you half your year to get around and 'lectioneer, and get elected for the next term.'

" 'Oh, it dont take much time, Dwight,' he said. Then, after a pause, he added, 'I got things pretty well organized.'

" 'But, Calvin, dont tell me that you can get elected without any effort.'

" 'Oh, I just let nature take its course.'

" 'Now, listen that's all right to tell everybody else, but you cant tell me you dont do something.'

" 'Well, maby I do nudge nature a little bit.' And he give one of his sly little grins as he admitted sorter helping nature out a bit.

"Did I ever tell you about one Sunday we was all at the White House and going to church, and somebody asked what time do we go? Coolidge answered immediately, 'Seven minutes to eleven at the elevator upstairs.' And that's when we went.

"Did I ever tell you how I got in with him at school in the first place? Well, I was from away out in Pittsburgh, and here I was at school right in the heart of New England, and I wanted to get right into the real atmosphere of New England and find a real New Englander; and out of all of them he was the only real New England atmosphere there was. The other New Englanders were not the type at all.

106

"Did I tell you about the time they nominated him at the Convention and was looking for a Vice President to run with him? Well, I was out there at Cleveland. Guess you was too, Will. I remember seeing you and Bryan sitting together at the Press stands.[8] Great old fellow, Bryan. Well, I was not much of a Politician, but on account of it being Coolidge that was to be nominated I thought I would go. I knew all the Leaders and was kinder on the inside. You remember what a time we had getting somebody for Vice President. It looked like we were going to have to draft the Janitor of the Convention Hall.

"Well, do you know why it was so hard to get one? It was Coolidge— we couldent get him to say who he wanted, and naturally Parties always try to nominate somebody that you wouldent mind being seen with.

"Then, as you remember, they went for Lowden. They even went so far as to nominate Lowden, but instead of making it final they adjourned till 8 o'clock that night till they could hear from him to see if it was O. K. Then he sent his famous Telegram: 'I have said I wont accept the Vice Presidency, and I cant go back on my word.' Then they hit on Dawes and put him over with a bang. But between each one of these nominations and proposed nominations they would phone to Coolidge at the White House and his answer would always be the same—'He is perfectly all right with me.'

"So, when the Convention was over and I got back to Washington, I said to Coolidge, 'Calvin, why dident you tell 'em who you wanted? It would have helped them out a lot.'

" 'No, I wasent going to tell 'em a thing,' he answered. 'I just let 'em use their own judgment picking a Vice President. Nobody told 'em four years ago and they did pretty well.' And another nice, quiet little grin from him.

"I dont know about him running again now, Will. You ask me if he has made any money from speculation. No, not a Cent. He aint the kind that would speculate, even if he wasent President. Of course, a President is supposed to have personal affairs the same as any of us, and what he does with his finances is none of our business. No doubt, he has some of his earnings invested in some good, solid bonds, but nothing of a speculative value that his administration might in some way be accused of helping in value. You know, he just dont look on money that way.

"Now, you take the way he has been raised. His great-grandfather had a Farm, and skimped and saved, and after a lifetime of work left it unincumbered, and a little nest egg of a couple thousand dollars. Then his son took it, and worked and saved, and left Coolidge's father perhaps eight or ten thousand. Then he works hard, saves and adds to that, and leaves Coolidge perhaps twenty-five or thirty thousand in addition to the farm. Now, that was progressive success. Each one took what he had, added to it, and left more than he started with. Coolidge will add to it and leave his son John quite a nice little fortune. Now, he can do that and when he dies he will know that he has carried out his mission: Live, work hard, be a good Citizen, and add to your savings.

"Here is another thing you can go back home, Will, and pretty near bet on. You wont see him messing into the following administration, if it should be Republican any more than if it happens to be Democratic. There will be none of the Roosevelt-Taft combination there. When he passes it on, it's ON.

"No, he said to me one time when he was kinder talking into the future, he said, 'This Country got along long before they ever heard of me, and they will get along long after I am forgotten.' You see, he has never lost his sense of proportion. He dont think that he is any greater than he was before he went in.

"Did I ever tell you about what my instructions were from President Coolidge when I come down here? Well, I couldent get anything out of him about just what I was to do, so finally I had to come right out and ask him. I was just about ready to go to the train, and here is what he said: 'Dwight, dont jump on Mexico. Just keep Mexico from jumping on us.' Now, it would be pretty hard to write a hundred-page Note to an Ambassador and give him any sounder advice than that. You know, he can say more things in less words than anybody.

"Then, another thing that Coolidge realizes better than anybody is this: He knows that he come into the Presidency from the Vice Presidency, where nothing is expected; he knows that he dident look like much when he arrived; he knows that even the Atheists, after looking him over, prayed for the salvation of the country. So he knows that anything that he did was a surprise, and he knows that he come into our public lives when we had had just about all the Government laws and advice that we needed. He saw that the less he did the more satisfied we would be with him.

"Well, it takes a smart fellow to do nothing, especially when you would perhaps look bigger at the time if you did do something. He knows that the next man that goes in cant get away with the same tactics. Every game and every Administration calls for different plans.

"Why, do you know even his personality (or what lots of them called Lack of Personality) was in his favor? You take one of those Office Seekers going in to see Harding or Taft or Roosevelt or any of those congenial fellows, and they had to be friendly and take up lots of their time. If they dident do that the old Office Seeker would come out sore. But with Coolidge, what they have heard and know of him, if they get in, and he even looks at 'em, why they think he has made a big concession, and are so tickled that they forget to ask about the office, they are in such a hurry to get out and tell their friends, 'Why he come pretty near shaking hands with me, and started to say "Hello!" Say, he aint a bad fellow at all. Where do they get that cold stuff?'

"That's why he has been able to physically stand the strain better. This reputation he has, has kept millions of pests away from him.

"No, I think you are wrong, Will, about him going to run again. Course, here is something he might do. Lay out for a while, and then? You see, his age will permit him doing that; he is not an old man, and wont be till several elections have passed, so just remember that in your predictions. And, say, we better go to bed; we got to get up early in the morning. Good night."

"Oh, say, Mr. Morrow, I see by the papers where Lindy is coming to Mexico. When is he coming?"[9]

"President Calles and I wired him to visit Mexico and we got an answer: 'Will be there the first clear day.' "

"Well, I better be getting out, 'cause he will be wanting my bed," I says.

I dident see the Morrows any more till a couple of months later when I saw them in Havana, during the Pan-American Conference, and Coolidge was there. Funny thing happened there that Mr. and Mrs. Morrow told my wife and me about. There was a big State Dinner given at the President of Cuba's Palace the night of Coolidge's arrival. The Coolidge's quarters were there in the same building. After the dinner was over and the guests were leaving, the Coolidges invited the Morrows up to their apartments. Well, they were up there talking so long and there was such confusion in the guests leaving that no one knew they were still there. When the Morrows went to leave, to go to their Hotel, the big old Palace was all dark and nobody knew how to get down. Coolidge was prowling around trying to show 'em some stairs. Then they couldent find their wraps, that had been left in the check room and it was shut up. Then they had to wake up the night watchman to get out. Coolidge said, "If this Palace is all located in Cuba, Cuba is bigger than you think."

When the big Battleship Texas steamed into Havana Harbor on that beautiful Sunday afternoon, and through thousands of cheering mobs the Coolidges were driven to this Palace, they were showed to their quarters. Coolidge dident pay any attention to any of it, then looked around and said to Jarvis, the head Secret Service man, "Where's the Baggage?"[10] During the hurrah of the welcome in a Foreign Country he wasent going to have some guy cop the old valise on him. The old days of coming into the Boston Station with an extra shirt in the bag in case the Legislature held over for a fall session was on his mind.

Course, one of the best ones was on last Inaugaration Day when he and Mrs. Coolidge was leaving for Northampton. It was raining cats and dogs, with thousands out in the rain. They got to the Station, got into their private car, and as they sit down he says to Mrs. Coolidge, "Grace, I bet a lot of 'em got wet today." And when he asked Mrs. Coolidge, when she was packing all her dresses, what she was going to do with them when they got to their house in Northampton, she said, "Why, I will put some of them in the cubboard."

"You better put 'em in the rooms and we will live in the cubboard," he says.

And when they got to Northampton that rainy morning, and the New Englanders were down to meet him after twenty-five years of splendid service, starting with being Mayor of that very town and winding up with running our Nation, well, there was a little band blowing away, and it's raining down their horns, and Mrs. Coolidge, rather overcome by her townfolks' reception, says, "Listen, Calvin, they are playing Home Sweet Home," and Mr. Coolidge replied, "Is it?"

Now, here is the last Morrow story I am going to give you. It was when he was up here just before Mr. Coolidge left the White House. He told it to me in my dressing-room. He is a guest at the White House and they are talking about this and that, and Coolidge remarked, "I just found out, our Government does do something in the way of a pension for its Ex-Presidents. We can send our letters for nothing. The only thing about it is, nobody wants to hear from us then."

A few nights ago, Everette Sanders, his very efficient and popular Private Secretary that served him so well at the White House, was back in my dressing-room and told this: It was in the morning about seven.[11] Coolidge is walking along the back of the White House and there is three men sitting on the lawn. "What are you fellows doing here?"

"Why, we are going to fix the boiler; we are just waiting till 7 o'clock."

"Oh, you are working here?"

"Yes, sir, Mr. President."

"Well, you better put out a sign then."

Oh, yes, I dident tell you the one that Morrow told me, about what he said about the Klan. The Ku Klux Klan argument was getting pretty hot in Politics and some of the papers was writing Editorials about what he should do about it. He told Morrow, "They put the Klan in Politics; now they want me to take it out."

Then, dont over look his famous one: "A lot of people think the war is over. The war aint over till the debt is paid."

Jim Wadsworth told me a good one.[12] He had to take one of these old busy Widows, that was promoting some Bill, for personal and publicity purposes, in to see the President.

She started right in trying to flatter him—"Why, Mr. Coolidge, you look much younger than your pictures give you credit for; there is much more color in your face than the Pictures show."

"Yes, guess I will have to change my Powder."

Well, this old Gal being all powdered and painted up, that knocked her back, but not out. She starts telling him about the Bill she wants indorsed—"in fact, Mr. Coolidge, your own State of Massachusetts I think endorsed it."

"Yes, I wrote it," and sure enough he had; he had introduced it himself up there years before.

Now, I wouldent have told you all these things, but he got to telling about himself in the magazines and I know he wouldent tell all. Course, I feel like I ought to give Morrow the check for this article, for he give me all the Stories, and if he needs it I will give it to him.

Course, to me the crowning achievement of Mr. Coolidge's entire career has been that he could find a House to rent for $42.50 a month. That's not Statesmanship, that's a Miracle.

Then, people ask you every day, "Has Coolidge got Humor?" Say, he has more real, downright, subtle humor than anyone we have in public life. We have had many little laughs at him and his rather eccentric ways while President, but for every one we have had at him, he has had a dozen at us. If he would sit down and write the funny things he saw while in there, then you would have a real masterpiece in humor. He saw 'em—dont forget that. Many a laugh those serious Senators must have handed him.

How to Be Funny

I have been interviewed in every Town in the United States, by serious-looking young College Boys, with horn-rimmed glasses and no hat, on the subject, "How would you advise a beginner to be funny?"

The interest they all show in it, you would think that all young America is practicing to be funny. I have tried to advise the Boys that I have known men in other walks of life that made more than Comedians. But its just one of the things that you cant discourage anyone from, once they have made up their minds. Its like these business men that go through life telling everybody they meet stories. The only novelty to it is that each man that tells it tells it worse than the fellow that just told you the same one down the street.

Now, you cant stop one of these fellows. Somebody laughed at him as a Boy, and it just practically ruined him. He is just doomed to go through life—"Did you hear this one? If you did, stop me." But these College Boys are aiming a little higher. They dont want to just repeat "The little Jewish fellow said to the Irishman." They have got their sights set on some humor. They are figureing on it for a profession. They figure that its like tending an Oil Station, that it is a profession that you can study and learn.

Some of these Boys when they come to interview me had their questions written out. About the best and most complete one was handed to me at Lincoln, Nebraska, where their State University is. I was playing there that night, and back stage come just about as dejected a looking Senior as I had ever seen. He was just about to finish school and was about to have to meet the world head on, and he wanted to be fortified with a profession. So he picked out humor, and he had from then to June to "Major" in it. He was matriculating in laughter at Bryans old stronghold. But he lost all confidence in me as a funny man when I couldent answer right off the reel the few little simple questions that he had written down and handed me. So I got him to let me take the paper and send him back the answers later.

American Magazine, September 1929

Now, here is his exact questions in the exact order he had them, and my answers:

"Is the field of humor crowded?"

Only when Congress is in session.

"What talent is necessary? Must one be born with a funnybone in his head?"

Its not a talent, its an affliction. If a funnybone is nessasary I would say that in the head is the place to have it. Thats the least used of a humorists equipment.

"Which offers the best field, the Essayist or the Humorist Feature Writer?"

Now, I dont know what an "Essayist" is. But if its one of those fellows that write what we used to call "Essays" at school, one of those recitations that you get up and speak, I am agin em. And as to the Humorous Feature Writer, just change that H to N and you have it.

"What field of Humor offers the best field now and which is most liable to develop?"

Well, I think the "Nut" or "Cuckoo" field is the best bet now, and from what I see of modern America, I think "Nuttier Still" or "Super Cuckoo" will be more apt to develop.

"In training what should one aim for?"

Aim for Mark Twain, even if you land with Mutt and Jeff.[1]

"Whats the best way to start being a Humorist?"

Recovery from a Mule kick is one thats used a lot. Being dropped head downward on a pavement in youth, has been responsible for a lot. And discharge from an Asylum for mental cases is almost sure fire.

"How should one practice for it after starting it?"

By reading Editorials in Tabloid Magazines and three pages of the Congressional Record before retiring every night.

"Should one jot down ideas?"

No! There will be so few that you can remember them.

"Should one read other Humorists?"

If you are Humorist, there is no other Humorist.

"Is it profitable to read other Humorists?"

Profitable but terribly discouraging.

"Do you think it does any good to play the Fool and wit at social gatherings?"

Not if they will feed you without it. But if you feel that you need the practice and just cant remain normal any longer, why go ahead. Everybody will perhaps want to kill you, and may. As for Social gatherings, I never knew of a Humorist getting into one if it had any social standing.

"Does College training add to your chances?"

Yes, nothing enhances a mans humor more than College. Colleges and Ford cars have been indespensible to humor.

"Should one specialize in any particular subject?"

Everything but English.

"What College would you suggest in preperation for a Humorous career?"

Harvard, if its present football continues.

"Must one have a heterogenous background of experience?"

You got me with that hetegenerous. But I will say "Yes" to that question and take a chance. I want to answer these 100%.

"Whats the best place to study human nature?"

At the source.

"Does a budding Humorist have to wait till he has acquired a philosophy?"

No, just a "Carona" typewriter is all.

"What is the precedure in submitting jokes or skits to Papers or Magazines?"

A return envelope stamped.

"Whats the best Magazine for amateurs?"

Ladies Home Journal.

"How do you get into Syndicate work?"

Lose all other jobs on a newspaper, or knock 50 home runs, or work 12 years with the Follies, and dodge all Literacy tests.

"Any advantage in Illustrating your own work?"

Yes, its the only way you can get it done right. Inferior Illustrators are spoiling our work.

"Do you think cartooning has a future?"

I certainly do. Its never had a boom, just a steady growth. The more we raise that cant read the more look at Pictures.

"Any demand for 'slangy' short stories on the style of Lardner and H. L. Mencken?"[2]

Yes, Lardners must sell. I saw him in Florida last winter with a stack of all Blue chips in front of him. Mencken has his own magazine where he uses what he cant sell.

"What Magazine would you send your first stories too?"

The nearest one.

"What's the oppurtunity of a good Gag man in the Movies?"

The oppurtunties are great, but the chances of getting in are small.

"Is there such a thing as running stale or getting out of material?"

I have heard of that happening, but in very rare cases. Every article seems better than the preceeding one, and continues so right up to the execution.

"Is it hard to get into Vaudeville, for a summer or a year?"

114

No, with all the different grades and classes of Vaudeville they have nowadays, its almost impossible to have an act so poor that somebody hasent got a Circuit that will fit you.

"This thing you do around the Country where you do a whole evenings entertainment yourself, just what is it?"

Son, I couldent tell you. With the oldtimers they called it a Lecture. With Politicians they call it a "Message." But with me its just a Graft.

"Is there any demand for Chalk talks?"

Not unless you are a Football coach.

"Is summer a bad time to start anything?"

If you want to make up your mind to start to be a Humorist, I believe I would wait till spring, if you can afford to lay off that long. Then if you should get disappointed, why you have a summer coming on instead of a winter.

"Mr. Rogers, could you tell me where I could be apt to sell this interview with you?"

No! But if you ever see it in print, I can give you a pretty good idea what Magazine might have used it.

The Grand Champion

Folks, I hate to brag. But it just looks like I have scored what Newspaper men call a "Beat" on all these other folks that make a success writing about people that have made a success. You know, we're getting to go in more every year for Champions, and "All Americans," and "Runners-up," and "Knockers-Down," and anything that really distinguishes you from the ordinary conglomerated hash of humanity.

We used to write about and look up to our rich men. But, sakes alive, we're getting so many now that no Magazine wont hold 'em. It takes Atlanta and all our combined Telephone Directories to hold the rich nowadays. Why, the rich is getting so common now that it's almost a novelty to be poor; and for a man to be pointed out as merely being "Rich" is just a kinda slurring way of saying he is ordinary. Then, too, everything is sold on credit anyhow, and there is really no inducement to be rich. You can get just as much static out of a Radio that has only had one payment made on it as one that come C. O. D. And even the most experienced cant tell by looking at a car how many payments are to be made on it. There is nothing that a rich man can do nowadays that a poor one cant follow and make a Sucker out of him. Why, the poor is even getting Golf Courses, so it's only a couple of years till they will be as big Liars as the rich.

Up to three years ago the poor thought it was against the law to gamble. Now they can tell you what General Motors closed at just as quick as a man that dont work for a living. Why, in the old days they thought if the price of wheat went up, it was because a bunch of Farmers' children had come home from boarding school and refused to eat Corn bread any more, thereby creating a bigger demand for flour. They dident know that it was because somebody (who dident even know whether it grew on a tree or you mined for it) had bought a million bushels which he would never see, or never move. But now that the little fellow has found out that he can buy a few bushels and not even have a wagon to haul it in, why, he has started to looking for something for nothing too.

So, outside of having the pleasure of learning etiquette from the Butler, the rich have practically no advantages over the poor. The poor have all the comforts, with none of the income taxes of the rich. What I am a-getting at is, you got to show something besides wealth to keep out of an obituary column that just reads, "Among those who died yesterday were."

Some rich men might just as well not die as far as the publicity they receive out of it is concerned. And it's a good thing too. It's making lots of rich kinda starting to repent in their later days. The trouble is it's so late then they can never give it back to the folks they got it from. It's kinda hard to tell just who to give it to, that it wont do about as much harm as if you had kept it yourself. A good many of the more ignorant rich give it to some form of higher education. The higher education goes, the more it teaches you how to live off the less fortunate. The smarter you get, the more disgraceful it is to manual labor. So all of our philanthropy has proven the real brains is in the disposing of money. There is a million dumb enough to make it, where there is not one smart enough to dispose of it so it will be a real benefit. You get it through good fortune, but to be of any good, it's got to be disposed of through *good judgment*.

A rich man has either got to make his name on what he did with his money or what he did for people in the way he was making it. If they feel he give 'em a run for their money, and really helped out his fellow man while alive, and tried to do something to make life a little more easy for him, why, then he is readily distinguishable from the herd. So I went into the common herd (that's right in with the rich majority) and picked me out a fellow that I am going to enter as my *Champion*.

Measured by the ordinary financial standards, he is not much shakes. I doubt if he knows what hour Wall street opens, or closes. He thinks Margins are the things you leave around the edge of anything. He knows what calling Hogs is; but Call Money would be Greek to him. He never did merge two or more Companies together and sell stock. He has had to make what little he has out of just what little he had to work with.

But, anyhow, we call a man a Champion if he is the best or head of any one thing. Bobby Jones is a Champion because he can find a hole in the ground quicker than a Prairie Dog.[1] Tunney, until he took up Shakespeare as a career and not as a recreation, was a Champion, because he could knock anybody Cuckoo before they could him. Houdini was the Champion of disappearing and appearing somewhere else.[2] Peggy Joyce has received more money for just saying "I Do" than Bacon got for being a silent Partner with Shakespeare and Co., Limited. (The limited was as to the amount of paper they had in those days.) So Peggy is a Champ in

117

her line. Between saying "I Do" and listening to Mendelssohn, her life has been nothing but Words and Music. Coolidge is a Champion; he never settled anything till it settled itself, which is wise. Hoover has fed more destitute than Childs.³ Mellon is a Champion. He took our Treasury when it was nothing but a building. Now it's a Vault. Al Smith is a second Columbus; he discovered 14 million Democrats in this Country when it was thought the race was practically extinct.

But what I am a-getting at is somebody that is more than a Champion in one or two lines. I want to show you a fellow that holds more records than all of the Champions put together. My man has had more influence on the lives, habits, and customs of the people of not only his own country, but all the World, than old Napoleon, or Cæsar, or any of those old Guys that happened to live in history because they destroyed all the books that dident have something about them. Cæsar ranted around down there in some little short hole country about the size of Pecos County, Texas. He kept a scrapbook, for he had a friend that was a critic. Shakespeare found the old scrapbook, and Amateur Dramatic Societies have played Roman plays when they ought to been playing Uncle Tom's Cabin. Napoleon was the originator of the Gang Leaders. He would have been a great Rum runner. He matched over 40 wars, and finished up only a Corporal. So he couldent 'a' been so much. From all the pictures I ever saw of him, he dident even know how to put his hat on straight. He always had it cockeyed, to keep the sun out of his ears instead of his eyes.

We get over into our own range and we find that Washington was quite a champion in three or four lines. We call him Father of our Country, because he never had a child. So that is really a kind of an honorary degree. He was a Surveyor and laid out the City of Washington with the hopes that no Senator would ever find the Capitol, and come pretty near succeeding. They have to go round so many Circles, that's what makes 'em act like Spinning Mice when they get there. George whipped England to try and get us Freedom; Canada stayed with England and got it. So it's sorta like Political speeches. It's always a question as to whether they are really an asset or a liability. So just really how much influence Washington has had on our lives, habits, and customs is sorta problematical. He made a record for truthfulness when his Father caught him with the tree down, Hatchet in his hand, and prespiration on his brow. He said, "Father, as much I detest circumstancial evidence, here is one case where it is true. I cut it down, and if I had it to do over again, I wouldent do it, for that is without a doubt the dullest hatchet in Virginia."

Lincoln heard about the record and advertising that Washington had received. So he says, "If that Guy with a white wig and knee Breeches can carve his way into the hearts of his countrymen with just a hatchet, give me an Ax and I will show you some chopping. Virginia might make Presidents, but out here in my country (wherever it was he was living) is the place to make rails." So he was quite a Champion, in more lines than one. He freed the slaves in the South but put the Southern whites in bondage for the duration of their natural lives. He gave Grant a box of Campaign Cigars, and poor Lee and his men had no Gas masks, so they had to surrender. Lincoln did all he could to prevent that war between the Democrats and the Republicans, and since then they have always settled their difficulties at the polls, instead of on the battlefield, and the results have always been the same, with the exception of an occasional accident, but when discovered it is always immediately rectified.

But the man I am about to name *("Go on and name him")* —As I said, the man I am about to name *("Name him")* —A Man who holds more records, been responsible for more things, changed the lives, habits, customs, and places of residence, has caused more laws to be made, more broken; in fact, just his influence in one day of our lives is more noticeable than what all the rest of our great men put together can show in a lifetime *("Name your Man")* —Well, Boys, it aint a soul but just our plain old friend, *Mr. Henry Ford.*

He is responsible for more things than any 100 other men of all time. Fifteen million things of one kind. Think of fifteen million of those things jumping out at you from every corner and crack of the civilized and uncivilized World.

Why, he has had more influence on the lives, habits, and customs of both man and beast than Andrew Jackson, Rupert Hughes, Webster, Charlie Chaplin, Nicholas Murray Butler, Lowell, or Thomas Heflin.[4] Many learned men made Laws (not learned laws, but Laws). Many misguided Souls have made Speeches. Preachers have copied down and offered up great Prayers. But no man ever moved humanity like Henry Ford.

Not only did he move 'em. But they knew they had been to a moving. Had there never been a Ford car, there would never have been a cheap car. It would have always been just classed as a rich man's Luxury. We all remember the time when everybody had it in for the man that come "honking" at us along the roads. We wouldent get out of his road. But the minute Ford made one that we could afford, and we was the one doing the "honking," why, that was different. Had the poor man never been able to get a car, he would never have voted good roads, and the things would have had a short fling and then passed out; for outside of wanting to be seen in a Linen Duster, Gauntlet Gloves, and Goggles, there was very little incentive, with the old roads, to own what they humorously called a car.

Will Rogers and Henry Ford at Dearborn, Michigan, with an Abraham Lincoln lookalike.

He, along with Brigham Young, is the originator of Mass Production. Just the very idea of thousands of things alike has had its influence on our Architecture, our dress, our minds. "Why think individually when all can think alike?" We started building our towns alike: Filling Stations on two corners and Drug Stores on the other two. You can pick up a block out of any town in America and sneak in and put it down in the night in another town, and it will be a month before anybody notices the difference. The whole thought of our Country has changed on account of him. We are thinking like a Ford. We assemble our education at a College just like they do a Car. You start through and each Teacher sticks a little something onto you as you go by their Department, the same thing on each one. When you get to the end, you get a Diploma like it does a license, and you all go out and start acting alike. The only difference is that Ford dont put anything on 'em that they aint going to use.

Then the ones of us out of schools are all thinking alike. If it hadent been for him we would all stay home and read or think for ourselves. Now we join a Luncheon Club, where the speeches are as much alike as the food and the Members. We use to kid the old Boys that sit around the Country Grocery Store and spit in the stove and settled the affairs of the Country on two good mouths-full of Battle Ax. But we aint a-producing anybody that can replace 'em. Them old boys mighta set and whittled. But their ideas were their own. They didnt get 'em from "The Speaker of today's Luncheon." You got to stay still to do much thinking. If you move like the other fellow, you will be thinking like him the first thing you know.

Course, everything you get you must pay for in one way or another. Cars made good roads. Good roads killed small towns. Small towns was where all our best thinkers come from. So cars havent been quite as cheap as we think they have. Paid Propagandists now do our thinking for us.

Henry Ford is responsible for more building than any man in the World. There is more money invested in Garages than in Schools and Churches. Every Automobile has a roof over it. Yet there is millions living in all ends of our Globe with the old Moon hitting 'em in the face all night.

Ninety-eight and one-half per cent of the building permits in small towns are for Filling Stations. Over two-thirds of the unemployed in this Country are working in Filling Stations.

If people slept in Filling Stations instead of just driving by them, it would solve the housing problem of this Country.

There is 300,000 men just pumping Gas into Cars every minute of the day in America alone.

193,000 just fixing Punctures.

800,000 just looking on; 750,000 of 'em offering advice, .009 successfully.

187,000 people every minute of the day just cranking the old ones; 81 with results.

Ford made a car that run with your feet instead of your head and hands. He was smart enough to know more people knew how to use their feet than they did their head or hands.

Why, there is 23,078 Ford radiators boiling over on the hills of this Country every day of every month, and think what that means in February, when Leap year comes and brings it to 29.

There is 43,000 just holding up the hoods of Fords looking at them, 42,598 with the same expression.

He is the only man that has made some change in the lives of everybody that ever come in contact with what he made.

A great Artist can paint a great Picture, and everybody that sees it might say "Great." But outside that it would mean nothing in their young lives. Great Teachers might have influence. But look at the millions and millions that they are not able to teach, and the other millions that they wouldent be able to learn 'em anything, even if they did teach 'em. But any time Henry Ford went out for the multitudes he either got 'em in it, or under it.

He has made more business for an Undertaker than any other one thing, with the exception of Prohibition. Monday morning after a beautiful, sunshiny Sunday finds the Undertaker singing at his work.

He has caused more people to go in debt than for rent or food.

He has drove more States, Counties, Towns, and Federal Governments in debt than the World War. We owe more for roads than we did to persuade the Germans to "please leave Belgium." Had we had no good roads we would miss all the scandal in the Highway Department; no State worries about who will be Governor. It's "Who will be on the Highway Commission?" I care not who writes a Nation's Songs; give me the Highway Contracts to deal out, and I will show you what hard work, perseverance, and taking advantage of your oppurtunities will do.

He has given us the biggest problem we have in America today, and that is, "Where am I going to park it?"

He has given us our second biggest problem we have today, namely, "After it's parked (and you come back and get it), how am I going to get home in it through the trafffic?" That's why so many people just leave 'em parked and turn Pedestrians for the balance of their normal lives.

But no matter where you build a road, Ford will fill it up for you. Even if you don't build one, his tracks will give you an idea where there should be one built. He has blocked up more roads than rains and landslides. He has taken the Police Force of the Towns off watching criminals and got 'em standing in the middle of the streets waving their arms. While the Police are holding up their right hand and blowing their whistle, the crook has held up your house and is blowing in your coin. He has taken more people more places where they have no business than all the rumors in the World.

Hoover fed the Belgiums. But it was Uncle Henry that give 'em a ride. He has pulled more expensive cars out of the mud than all the mules and horses combined. He took ahold of Detroit when it was a one-night stand and made a week out of it. A Ford and Charlie Chaplin are the two best-known objects in the World today.

Chinamen that don't know where their next Missionary is coming from can pour a couple of quarts of rice in the thing, and it will run. It's as well known with Englishmen as a Teapot; and Zulus that never heard of Farmer's relief can take one down and get enough of it back together again to run. A Nicaraguan thinks "a Ford Car, a Machine Gun, and a bevy of Marines" is our only three products we make.

Edison has been great; he gave us the Electric light. But Ford fixed it so we woulden't have to stay home at night and use it. I don't know who give us the radio announcer, but bless Ford for getting us out of hearing of him. Columbus discovered a new World, but the old Tin Lizzie has made us discover America.

He has had more jokes told about his car than the 1924 Democratic Convention. He has fixed it so the poor can go as fast as the rich, especially if you get in front of him on a narrow road. He has been responsible for thousands of men getting rich by just making things that go onto Fords after they are supposed to be finished. He is the only man that ever shut four hundred million dollars' worth of Plants and equipment down for six months and never looked a Sheriff in the face, or had to go to Town and renew his Notes. He takes America to town every day, sometimes twice. He has made it possible for City people to see a Cow— maby hit her. He has scared more horses than a Steam Calliope and Elephants combined, and caused more runaways than Tumbleweeds.

He was the first person interested enough in Art to further "Old-time Fiddling." He was the first rich man to discover that an old-time fiddler could play just as good as a long-haired one with a Foreign name and a missfit dress suit. There never was a Foreign Fiddler yet that ever played that could make an audience pat its foot; and there never was an audience that ever heard a Country Fiddler play that could keep from patting it.

He done more to further Aviation than all other rich men combined. So the Champion of all Champions should be called THE GRAND CHAMPION. So that's what I enter him as.

Course, if you want a few more statistics and facts, why, here they are:

123

He has cause more dirty dishes to be left in the sink after supper than all of the Leading men in the Movies.

He has broke more people's wrists than all the Osteopaths in the World combined.

And caused more Profanity than Congress and Senate combined.

First man to discover every Joke sold a Car, and every Joke bought one.

Broke in more customers for other cars than necessity.

Only Millionaire that ever apoloized for ANYTHING.

Gives more value for the least money. A Marriage certificate and a Ford Car are the two cheapest things known. Both lead to an ambition for something better.

IT COST HIM ONE HUNDRED AND FIFTY MILLION TO GET AMERICA OUT OF ONE FORD AND INTO ANOTHER.

124

Corn Whiskey
Courage and Commerce

We have got a serious situation confronting us with this liquor problem. They are smuggling thousands of cases of American (so-called)
liquor out of this country every day. Foreign countries have taken to our
liquor because it is so different from anything they ever tasted in their
lives. Our Government is just beginning to realize how much we have
lost on export duty alone, so now we are sending our fleets to chase their
boats away, and to try and check this flow of American-made (so-called)
liquor into Europe.

If our Congress had had the good of the American people at heart
instead of just the raising of their own salaries, and put a good, stiff
export duty on this American-made (so-called) liquor, in the next few
years we could have paid off our National Debt. But, like everything else,
Congress was slow to realize what an industry we've got. When it first
started in August, '18, with just a few scattering stills, little did we dream
that we were witnessing the birth of a new industry. Like everything else
new, everybody said, "It won't work." They have said the same about
every great movement. Why, the first airship to leave the ground, there
was even doubt as to whether they could get it down again. Even Henry
Ford was ridiculed when he first predicted that he could block the traffic
of a Nation continuously. But now these two scientific achievements are
taken by everybody as an everyday occurrence.

From this humble beginning of this American-made (so-called) liquor
it has grown and grown until now we proudly boast of it as our fifth
largest industry. Automatic pistols are first, burglar tools second, stolen
automobiles third, hot dogs fourth, American-made (so-called) liquor
fifth, coffins for gunmen sixth, cigarettes seventh, English Lectures
eighth, and nose powder ninth. At first it was thought to be only a thing

American Magazine, May 1930

for home consumption, and little did we think it would ever have Foreign possibilities.

Europeans are born and raised on beer and wine. They have it at their tables at every meal, the same as Alabama has quinine. Europeans have been accustomed all their lives to drink all they want, sometimes for hours at a time, and then get up and walk home, even in narrow streets. Headaches were as foreign to them as bathtubs. But came a day after the war when there was an exchange of travel among all the countries. Foreigners arrived here and began to partake of our new hospitality. They soon realized that one drink of our National weapon carried more real authority than a hogshead of beer and a flagon of wine, and that two drinks called for a rehearsal of the late war. Never before in their lives had they ever experienced the sensation of unconsciousness without an anesthetic, so they began to inquire what manner of libation or concoction is this odd drink, and could some be procured to take back to the various Fatherlands (which was, by the way, the first start of International Bootlegging).

Various bottles of this having reached other countries, after trials and tests it was found to cause almost the performing of miracles. So they took it to their scientists and their chemists to find what it contained. But at last we got even with Einstein. They knew no more of OUR THEORY than we did of his. Finally, America had made one thing that Europe couldn't duplicate cheaper. One of the most learned of their chemists, after dissecting it for months, finally got discouraged and drank it, and, unfortunately for his family, wasn't insured. What made it so discouraging to try and assay the contents was that after they thought they had discovered the odd ingredients of one bottle, the next one they examined would be found to contain none of the elements of the first one.

After examining thousands of bottles from various parts of America, the only two things they found that any two bottles had in common were that it all flowed and that death was inevitable. But between the time of drinking and the hour of demising they began to realize its possibilities as a courage builder. Why breed courage into a race, which takes generations, when you can buy it out of a bottle? For, instead of returning peacefully to their homes, as had been their custom on their various national drinks, after taking one shot of American corn they have been known to meet a street car head on purposely, and instead of paying a taxi-driver, they would just whip him and confiscate his car. So they started ships to our shores to procure cargoes of this unfathomable ingredient. But they were not allowed to openly dock and receive their wares.

The law first said they could only come within three miles, so boats

126

began stealing out into the night from the mosquito-tracked shores of Long Island and New Jersey like Pirates of Old, only these were carrying a more precious contraband. Then it was that the authorities first began to realize the seriousness of the situation. So they moved them out to a twelve-mile limit. International Marine Law didn't designate twelve miles, but what is nine miles more between supposedly peaceful Nations?

As this alleged fluid began to arrive in European countries in quantities, queer things began to happen. Some unlearned men blamed these odd happenings to what they called "After-War Conditions." But the local Confuciuses knew the real cause was the arrival of this American liquid radium.

Just one case of Kentucky Mountain Dew fell into the hands of the Moroccans, and before the case was half empty they pounced on Spain like a Bulldog. In killing the last quart (which was mutual between the liquid and the consumer), the Leader took two swigs and says, "Bring on France. Why have a war that is one-sided?" Just one bottle reached the throats of the Armenians and they refused to tip their hats to the Turks.

Even such a Dignitary as the Prince of Wales, after being refreshed from an Oklahoma recipe from the private still of Joshua Cosden, went back home and told George and Mary "to pick 'em out another boy, that the King business didn't interest him in the least."[1]

And just to think, this is the industry that our Government is trying to kill off. The only real, strictly American invention since chewing gum. You take away our foreign markets on liquor and you will find it will bring a hardship on this country. There would be thousands of "stills" that would have to close. We're hollering for more Agricultural legislation "To Protect the Tiller." What about the Stiller? Let's not have privileged legislation. I think all Nations should be allowed to have all they want of our American-made (so-called) liquor, because at the rate we are drinking it here, and the effects it is having, why go crazy alone? Let's feed it to the world, and we'll all GO CUCKOO TOGETHER!

The World's Best Loser
Why I'm Pulling for Sir Thomas to Lift That Cup

If you asked a thousand people who would they consider the most popular person, regardless of Nationality, sex, or size, in the whole World, just I mean absolutely popular on account of their oustanding personality—well, as answers you would get Lindbergh, the Prince of Wales, and Charlie Chaplin. Mr. Hoover is well known all over the World and popular. Women—there is no outstanding woman personality that's known all over, with the exception of Lady Astor.[1] I don't mean just some prominent person like a King, that they would just want to see on account of the novelty. I mean somebody that's liked and really admired, everywhere they go. Well, you couldent guess it in a week, and I bet you will agree with me when I name him. It's Sir Thomas Lipton.

I defy anyone to name not only a more universally liked, but loved Character than old Sir Thomas. I have had him in my audience in London, and many, many times over a course of years in New York, and he has never failed to get the biggest hand (not a hand but an ovation) than anyone I ever introduced.

And it's that way everywhere. I saw him last in Los Angeles and everybody brightens up and smiles when they see him. He has traveled over the world much more than any of the others that I mentioned. He is at home in any Country, makes speeches and tells his jokes in all gatherings to all nationalities. He is bringing a boat over to race us again this year. Now, what sporting event could you mention in any Country in the world where the home Country would be pulling for the "Foreigner?" But there will be more Americans pulling for him to grab that "vase" than pulled for Lindy to outwit the Reporters at the wedding.

You got to have something besides just "Good Sportsmanship" to win popular approval like that. So that's why I claim the Title for him of "World's Sweetheart." Sounds kinda effiminate, but it's really the only

American Magazine, September 1930

Title that will fit. The old Rascal was always a great favorite with the Ladies and he has been called Sweetheart by more Women than any other man. And men all over the World have always referred to him as a "Regular Guy," which makes him sorta the sweetheart of them. So the World's greatest Sweetheart is really not a Woman at all, but an old Man.

I opened at the Pavilion Theater in London in the summer of '26, and he and his old Crony, Lord Dewar, who has since died, were there in a Box.[2] Dewar was the greatest after-dinner Speaker in London. Well, I introduced them to the audience and we had a lot of kidding back and forth with each other, from the stage to the box. Englishmen had never seen a performer have the audacity to point anyone out in an audience, and they perhaps were more shocked than amused.

Lord Dewar had the finest stable of race horses in England and raised the finest Dogs. He give me a dog. The children brought the dog home and we got him now. Put him in a dog show after Lord Dewar saying he was the best of that breed in England (Sealingham). He won second and I cabled Dewar, "Dog won second if you had given me a good one I would have won first."

But let's let Sir Thomas tell some. I had a whole evening with him not long ago at a little Dinner given in Los Angeles by Mr. Schaffer, the Newspaper owner and an old friend of Sir Thomas'es.[3] There was just he and the Host and Mrs. Schaffer and Mrs. Rogers, and Miss Hart from New Orleans. It was a lovely dinner and we just sit there and made a whole evening of it, as Sir Thomas was going great.

I've entertained on my Yachts, he says, at various times all over the World every King and Queen and High Potentate there has been in my time; and did you know that I landed at Castle Garden as a boy, an immigrant, right here in your own country? Oh, I know your country better than you know it. I made a few shillings on the boat coming over by being able to write some letters for others that couldent write. We were all steerage passengers. Then, when I landed, I got free room and board at a little Hotel away downtown in New York, by bringing to that hotel twelve others who paid. I was to bring twelve and I dug up thirteen for fear one would run out on me.

I worked at everything under the sun, all over this great Country of yours. I was down in Virginia, around Charleston, into Tennessee a great deal; then to New Orleans. I saved up enough to get home from New Orleans, and also enough to take me Mother a present, and what do you think it was? You could never guess. It was a rocking chair. I wanted to see her sit and rock and rest. And I also took her a barrell of flour. Just think, to eat and rock. The old Merchant sold me the flour cheap when I told him what I was doing with it, that it was a present for me old Mother.

Did you know I was the fourth person ever was given the freedom of the City of Glascow? The Prince of Wales, the Duke of York, and the Duchess of York, and then your "Uncle Tommy." The "Great Sir Thomas Lipton" they was calling me. "Great" me eye. They was calling me great when here I had worked in Glascow for half a crown a week. And some of 'em in the crowd knew me when I did it. So I couldent put on any of me "Lugs" with them. I used to bring me Mother home the half Crown and tell her some day I will have more horses and carriages for you to use than you will know what to do with, and she lived to have 'em too, plenty of 'em.

I had her a big, fine home five miles outside Glascow and now that home is the Glascow Memorial Home for Nurses. Dont you think that would please me Mother if she knew it? I go out to see 'em all the time. And at my big celebration at Glascow for me, I told 'em that any Boy could get up in the World if he only used his Mother as his guiding spirit. She has been my inspiration all my life, and there has never been a night that I layed down that you wont find the picture of her the nearest thing to my pillow. If you will go with me to my Hotel now, I will show it to you.

And, oh, how poor we were when I was a boy. We were Poor and Irish —and that's as poor as you can get. A poor Irishman is the poorest thing there is; they never do anything in halves. We were Irish but we lived in Scotland; I was born and raised in Glascow. All my boats have had Irish names, the various "Shamrocks," and my Yacht the "Erin" is the one I cruise on.

During the war I fitted it up as a Hospital Ship, and stayed on it and run it myself. We had some great experiences, I can tell you; we were mostly down in the Mediterranian and the Adriatic. Your American Doctors and Nurses did some great work in some of those Countries, like Serbia, Bulgaria, and Greece. Long before you was in the war they were helping out down there. They had 14 Hospitals established down there. I have seen 'em in Belgrade when the Patients, the Doctors, and the Nurses all had Typhus. The dead was among the living.

And the first thing they asked me for when I come in with my Hospital Yacht, what do you think it was? It was for an American Flag. They said they were being fired on at various times and they thought that Flag flying over would help to prevent it. I gave 'em one, and later the head Doctor, a very wonderful American, died, and he told 'em to telegraph me for another Flag, and I took 'em one. He had asked to be wrapped up and buried in the other one. We were fired on many times, mostly by Submarines. We had some great experiences.

But never mind that. We wont dwell on those most unfortunate times.

130

We are here to be merry, and Sir Thomas is always merry. Ah, we have had some merry times on the old "Erin," I can tell you.

Did I ever tell you about the time that we were on a pleasure cruise and I had some of the biggest "Toffs" in England on board? Among them were four "Highnesses." Three of them were Royal Highnesses, and the other just a Highness. I got the morning Paper and it said the King of Spain was to visit England.[4] So they all set to talking about him, and I told the Girls to get ready to set their caps for him, that a real honest-to-goodness King was in the offing. Well, the one that wasent a Royal Highness, but just a Highness, was a fine, dashing young Lassie, and I told her in particular to go after the King. She felt that she wouldent have the same chance as the others on account of her rank, but I told her she would have the best chance. I knew the King and I knew her, and she is the one that did it. She is today the Queen of Spain, and I see 'em often when I go there, and I joke her about it.

Oh, I have some good times in my life, I can tell you. I hope I have a lot of friends everywhere; I know I like 'em all. It's said that I have been given the freedom of more Cities than any other human. If I carried all me Keys with me that I have, you would take me for the Warden of the Tower of London. The freedom of the great city of New York was presented to me before seventy thousand people, and they give me an American Flag. But it was no better than that first trip when I landed here as an immigrant boy of seventeen.

In the midst of the New York celebration a man edged his way to me and asked me if I wasent the boy that stopped at his hotel free and eat so many Pan cakes. He had me right, I couldent "High-hat" him; he knew me when I was just a Pan cake eater. I had never had any, and I thought they were the best things I ever tasted.

Ah, many of your Cities have been good to me. I get what you Americans call a "Kick" when I hear someone say that's the "Famous Lipton." The Kick comes because they dont know that I dont take the whole thing serious. "Famous Lipton"—I am an immigrant and will always be an immigrant. "Famous" me eye.

Did I ever tell you about the time we were on a pleasure cruise down around Italy? There was a lot of Swells, Earls and Dukes, the Lord Mayor of London, and one big German Notable. Well, we were in a little out-of-the way Port, and the German ashore run onto some of his own Country-men; and he asked if he might not invite them aboard, and they come for lunch. They dident really know who any of us were; the German hadent told them. But as they were going ashore the Lord Mayor couldent stand it any longer; he wanted them to know who they had dined with. Not just a lot of people, but some real "Folks." Well, he told 'em, and the German Tourists looked at him as though he was crazy and said, "Yes, that's a great story, but we knew you all the time. You are a moving Picture troop, and those are the parts you are playing. The German fellow that asked us aboard, he is the Manager, and as for you being the Lord Mayor (he was a little fellow), why, you are not big enough. (In Germany it seems all the Mayors are big physically.) You couldent even be a Justice of the Peace, and as for the tall old fellow with the Steward's cap on that you called 'Lipton,' he is just the Waiter."

Did I ever tell you about the time I sold me packing plant to Ogden Armour?[5] It started from my pork business. Dident you know that at one time I had the corner on pork in this very Country of yours? Why, yes, I was going to put into our Tea stores Bacon, so I build a big plant in Omaha and start in buying pork. Papers all come out and said, "Thomas Lipton corners the Hog market, makes five million." Dident make a cent; I even lost money. But I dident tell them so. I just let 'em think: the great Lipton is smart. Smart me eye; they took me last pig away from me.

Well, I had this Pork packing plant on my hands and I tried to sell it to Ogden Armour. He said, "I wouldent have the thing as a gift." Well, that made me mad. So I started to scheme.

Finally I got hold of a man that was the best Manager of Beef Packing Plants in the Country. I asked him if he dident think a trip to Europe would do him good, all expenses, money besides, and all he had to do was to let me use his name as having gone to work for me, in my new "Beef Packing Business" which we would open in addition to the Pork business, and that I dident care how loud he broadcasted the fact in Europe.

Well, there must have been no Static in his announcement in Europe (you see, Armour was then in Europe), and the Cables begin to burn to ask what I would take for the plant. I was a-getting offers from all of them. But Armour was the one I was laying for, and he is the one that I landed at just exactly five times the amount that he could have bought it at the time he "wouldent have it as a gift." And I had no more ideas about packing beef than I have of swinging that rope of yours, Will.

Did I tell you about the time that "Honey Fitzgerald," the "Sweet Adeline" Mayor of Boston, made the King and Queen of England wait?[6] I must tell you. Well, it was down at the regatta at Cowes. Fitz wanted to come down and see me on my Yacht, so he come to the landing near where I was anchored out in the bay, and he saw a Launch there. He dident know it was the King's; he dident know who's it was. But he was all dressed up like a man from Boston would be that was getting on a Yacht for the first time, and his Lovely Daughters were with him; and very important he said, "Take me to Sir Thomas Lipton's Yacht." Well, it was so commanding that they thought perhaps it was some important friend or Guests of the King's, so they took him out to us. When they arrived he paid the man half a Crown, and here the King and Queen had come to the landing in the meantime and Fitz was using their Launch, so they had to dangle their feet in the water till Fitz sent it back.

Did I ever tell you about the time I was in the newspaper business, Schaffer? Well, I was motoring from the south of France, and Lord Dewar come along to keep from paying train fare, and we got to Calais. I sent Dewar to buy some English papers and get the news. He brought a bunch back and I had 'em all on my lap, and a man saw them and asked, "Have you the London Gazette?" I said, "No, but I got the Main, the Express, and any of the others." He picked out one and asked me "How much?" I told him "Tuppence." He gave me the two pennies, and when Lord Dewar returned I told him I had taken one of his investments and made 100% on it, as I knew it only sold for one penny in London. "You sold it for Tuppence, eh?" Well, I give Thrippence for it here in France, so you lost me 100%. It's a good thing you do your business with people that dont know the difference from good or bad, or you would be a Bankrupt."

Lipton is 80 years old, as strong and well as a two-year-old. Never married; been engaged to every Woman, he says, since "Cleopatra;" has been called a "Perfect Dear" by all of them. Has been introduced at Banquets from Ceylon to Seattle; from Bombay to Beverly he has heard them arise and sing "For he is a jolly good fellow."

He is great old man; he should be a lesson to the World. Here is a man that does business in every corner of the World, and they all love him and he gets along with all of them. The World could learn much from the old Sea Dog, this Real Sportsman, THE WORLD'S BEST LOSER.

Quien Sabe Caramba?
By Will Rogers
"Delegate-at-Large"

Well, the rest of you can freeze for dear old Kiwanis if you want to, but I will keep my overcoat on. I have been sitting back there shivering long enough. I am not going to do it any more. I am going to be comfortable.

Well, let me see. Oh, yes, about this guy here (President Endicott).[1] I may be slipping in public estimation, and in various ways, but I never thought I would reach the stage, especially in this particular year, when I would be introduced at an affair by a banker. He is associated with us here, but if he thinks it is through mutual friendship I want to tell him it is on account of old friendship and not new.

I am going to be a terrible disappointment here tonight. You have already had two principal speakers. I have heard them. I am going to be a flop here because I cannot recite a bit of poetry and never could in my life. But I have some little pamphlets that I will hand out to you later!

I have seen a good demonstration of memory here tonight, not only by the speakers, but that guy (Secretary Parker) who introduced everybody.[2] I don't know these people up here on the stand, but if you don't mind me taking up a little of your time I would like to introduce the audience to you!

Laying all joking aside, that old boy did a good job in introducing the speakers, even if we didn't know whether he was introducing them right or not!

I want to compliment the Kiwanis Singers. They tell me they gathered here from the various parts of the state. Many of them, of course, are from Southern California. They just met here to sing. Well, you could tell that. They did right well. They had the words before them and most of them finished at the same time.

This occasion has given me the opportunity to come here in this canyon. I live in another canyon over yonder. I live in a bigger and better

Kiwanis Magazine, official publication of Kiwanis International, August 1933

Will Rogers hosted several officials of the International Kiwanis Convention at the Fox studio in June of 1933. Front row: Mrs. Morton S. Hoiss, Rogers, H. G. Hatfield, Fred C. W. Parker, and Walter R. Weiser. Back row: Mrs. H. G. Hatfield, Mrs. Carl E. Endicott, Mrs. Fred C. W. Parker, Carl E. Endicott, Mrs. J. Clark Sellers, J. Clark Sellers, Mrs. Ben G. Wright, and Ben G. Wright.

canyon than this one. This is the first time I have ever been in here. I want to thank you all for getting me in because this particular Bowl was dedicated to art and rattlesnakes. This is very artistic here. All Hollywood is highbrow and how the devil you all got in here is more than I know!

On account of this being a nice cool night I do not want you ladies to be afraid of the rattlesnakes. They are kind of chilly tonight and will not bother you. But do not drop in here on a hot afternoon. I am telling you!

I am glad to be here. I enjoyed the speakers very much, even if I didn't know who the poet was. But I did enjoy that old boy—I don't know his name—the old bald-headed guy—the Huey Long of Kiwanis.[3] (indicating Roe Fulkerson)—I can tell he could speak at the drop of a hat and he was ready to drop it.[4] He made a good speech. He writes for that splendid *Kiwanis Magazine*. That is the Congressional Record of Kiwanis. He made a dandy talk.

"Quo Vadis?" You have got to have a subject when you speak nowadays. "Whither goest thou?" Now, I don't know anything about Latin, but I do know a few Mexican words. My address tonight is going to be called "Quien sabe caramba?" If you are not familiar with Mexican, "Quien sabe caramba?" means "Who the hell knows?"

My friend, Roe, spoke of the library back there. When he went up in that wonderful library, where he gets all these gags, I thought he was talking about the Congressional Library. Congress found out that 800 people worked in it and further that 760 of them are Republicans. The Democrats are going to do something about it. They are going to try to get these Republcans out of there. They claim it is a total loss having the Republicans in there, but if the Democrats get in it would be beneficial. You didn't know there were 800 people working in the Congressional Library—I mean paid to be there? Well, that is what the paper said. I only know what I read in the paper. Well, I thought Roe was going to bring that up when he spoke about the library.

About this other fellow, the advertising man, Bruce Baxter.[5] I enjoyed his talk too. He sort of advertised education and religion. He made a dandy talk too, the same one I have heard him make at other clubs! He speaks at all these commencement exercises around here. I have read his addresses at graduating exercises. These boys start out into the world, after finishing school, with nothing. It used to be that they could get a job working in a filling station but they cannot do that any more. That is very exciting work because they were liable to be robbed at any time, and generally by another fraternity brother!

I am here tonight as kind of a peace offering. I have told a lot of jokes about these eating outfits, service clubs, or whatever you want to call them.

One of the speakers tried to alibi the idea that this wasn't a luncheon club. He said that they came about through necessity. They came about at a time when everybody in America was joining something. Do you remember that? There was a time in your life, a few years ago, when you could run around with an application and say, "Here, boys, join this." And then when you would ask him what he had joined he would say, "I don't know. It is just to eat away from home. That is all I know about it." Everybody in the country belonged to everything but their own family.

I have told a lot of jokes about these service clubs, or eating outfits, because I could not see much sense in them. But they were beneficial to the hotels because they got rid of a lot of bad food.

I remember one time, up in Frisco, when I spoke before one of these clubs. There were a lot of speakers on the program. The president of the club said, "We must get out of here right on time. I want to run everything on time." At first he told me I could have ten minutes. Another one of the speakers, the chief of police, got up and spoke ahead of me and he could not get him stopped. Finally, he turned to me and said, "You will have only eight minutes now." The chief kept on talking and the president of the club said, "You will have only six minutes now. I will step on your foot one minute before your time is up."

When I got up to talk I said, "Well, I have been to these service club outfits, luncheon clubs, all my life but never before did I know what one of them was formed for." I could see no reason for them. But that day I found a reason—he had to let them out by a certain time. He said, "We must be out by 1:30. We had trouble last year every time we ran over." I told them that I was first given ten minutes, then eight minutes, and then it finally got down to six minutes. I told them the president was to step on my foot one minute before my time was up to be sure that I would not run over. Then I said, "I am going to help him out today more than any of the speakers. He has given me six minutes to talk and he is going to step on my foot one minute before my time is up. Now I have found out what a service club is really organized for—it is for the sole purpose of getting you out of here at 1:30 and I am going to give him back five minutes and you are going to be out five minutes earlier."

All of that was back in the old days. It looks like you have really got a mission to fulfill now; you are doing something. I imagine in all the different towns you have got away from the luncheon club idea, but when you first broke out you were terrible. You deserved all the kidding that you got. But now you have reformed and you are going along all right. I know from personal experience that you are getting along fine and doing something worth while.

That is about all I can think of to say that would be any good for you. Now don't let this fog worry you because it will be just as bad

137

tomorrow. It is not unusual at all. We have had it for two months here. This is the clearest night I have seen in weeks!

I don't know as I have any news for you. I thought I was going to have some news. The baby was a hoax. When I heard Aimee had a baby I kind of felt encouraged.[6] Well, we must not tell too many jokes about Aimee because, although she does some foolish things, she also does a lot of good things.

Another gentleman we have here, and who is a public character, is Mr. Shuler.[7] I don't tell jokes about him. I do not want that gentleman going into the Baptist Church some night digging up any of my early records. Me and Mr. Shuler have a working agreement. We lay off each other.

On account of this wonderful structure in this canyon being dedicated to art, and no politics is allowed to enter here, I would like to tell you how to vote tomorrow. If you want a drink just vote "yes," on whatever proposition it is. Tomorrow is election day. You can vote here in Los Angeles. You do not have to be here for a long time like you do in some places. That is why there are so many people out here. You know, they stop the trains here and take the census. You know what I mean. If you are registered on your hotel register here that is all that is necessary and it will entitle you to vote.

I hope the town is treating you all right.

We have the name of being windy and doing a lot of foolish things. The air races will come off here pretty soon. This is the right place to hold the air races. We have more air here than in any other city in the world! We ought to be able to put on a good air race. We ought to encourage the air races because future wars are going to be fought in the air. Nobody will hand you a gun in the next war. They are going to slip you an airplane and tell you to go aloft and see if you can come down.

You know, Mr. President, I am to report as to the condition of the country. I report progress on account of the Democrats being in.

I was a Democrat before it was fashionable. I was a Democrat when they thought something was the matter with you for being one. You know why I am a Democrat? Because they have no humor. You have got to have more than humor to be a Democrat. They really are getting along fine now.

You cannot find a Republican anywhere these days. I stopped off at the world's Fair in Chicago the other day. The biggest exhibit they have there is that they are showing a Republican.

PREVIOUSLY
UNPUBLISHED
ARTICLES

"Wrote for 5th Ave. Association—
Never Used"

I see where 5th Avanus is celebrating its One hundredth birthday. I dont know how old these other Avanues are. They have no association so I doubt if they get any credit at all for being in NY.

Since this 5th Avanue Association has been in existence, the Avanue has made remarkable progress. From 23rd to 34th, where in the days there was no 5th Avanue Association to chart its destiny, why all they had was such unknown joints as the 5th Avanue Hotel and the Hoffman House, Markins Restaurant, now all that has been replaced with high class Artistic Button Hole Factories, and basting establishments. Moving Picture Companies use it now as a location around 12 oclock midday to take Pictures where the locale is supposed to be St Petersburg or Moscow. There hasent been a word of English spoken on 5th Ave below 34th in three years.

Even the Waldorf Hotel nobody is stoping there but Democrats, and its only 2 years until they will be all practically out of existence. Where (so and So Restaurant was) they now have a hot dog stand. The traffic Policemen down there are paid in Lyres.

From 34th to 59th where used to be located only the beautiful homes of our Millionaires, why now it has all exclusive shops, 5 Woolworth 5 and 10 cent stores, the competition between them and Kresse is something startling.

Hannans exclusive shoe store, he has 12 of them, so they are sure to have a pair will fit you if you have the time.[1]

Tiffany is on 5th Avanue but they havent sold a Diamond since Peggy Joices last wedding.

All upstairs are occupied by Ex Ray machines, to tell you whether it is Pyorehea or Lampers you have.

Spaldings Sporting Goods store has sold out. Woolworths have taken over all the sporting goods trade being done on the avanue.

If a man from Park Avanue was caught on 5th Avanue he would be arrested for slumming.

They have towers all along the street.[2] It is the first street in A[blank] to look like the New York Central after it electrocuted itsself and put in Towers.

We will always keep it as it will be valuable to parade on. I have always maintained that one street in every town should be set aside just to parade on, then let people go there to see it.

What few 5th Avanue homes are still in existence, the property is in an Estate and the heirs cant give a clear Title.

It is more crossed than any street in the World. Everybody is trying to get either on some Avanue east of it or west of it, crossed by traffic.

Horn and Hardart are negoiting for the site where the Library is.[3] Since Radio come in nobody has taken a book out of there.

Nobody can cross the stret. This Association was formed by men who have survived crossing the Ave., thats all that is nessary to membership. I think this Committee can well report progress.

Idea on Piece for Liberty

Its not often that Ye Olde Reliable Editor, Of Ye Olde (more) reliable Illiterate Digest consents to pen an Editorial for an outside Journal of learning. But after all there is a certain courtesy that one Editor owes to another, and when your Editor invited me as Guest Editor to contribute, I immediately did so, For in return I may some time have an open space in my weekly harangue, and feel that some little small bore talk talk will fit in, he will come in handy to me. Of course I wouldent trust him on any questions of the day, But some frothy little robbery or divorce where it wouldent mean anything to our Policy would be all right. Everybody was astounded when this Magazine gave $50.000 for just the suggestion of the Title, "Liberty," But that was cheap for "Liberty,"[1] America owes $30,000,000,000 (thats Billions Bub, NOT Millions) It owes that much mostly FOR Liberty, and we havent got our deeds exactly straight yet. Its are kinder like our Movie Stars husband's Title. Its clouded, or still in Escrow.

We all love Liberty, I guess its because we get so little of it. France gave us a Statue representing Liberty, But it had its back turned on us, and couldent see whether we were getting any of it or not. It represents four billion, four hundred million, (and some odd cents) to us now. France now says our hearts are as hard as the Ladys right arm that holds the Lamp, and nobody has been gentlemanly enough to take it from her for all these years.

As the great Ex-Statesman from Oklahoma, Isac Walton said, "Give me Liberty or give me the Saturday Evening Post."[2]

"Liberty" should be in every home especially if there is a husband there. So if four million of our boys are always ready to fight for it, I can certainly drop my worthwhile work long enough to write for it.

But away with Liberty, why speak of the millinium. Away with everything, and onto the question at hand. I am as long getting to my subject as an After Dinner Speaker. With this exception, I will get to mine. Liberty's Editor wants to know how it feels to go from Zeigfelds Follies to the "Lecture Platform," From a Tax exempt audience to Tax Payers. "From Foolights to Rostrum," "From Bootleggers to Boot wearers," "From National Folly's to State Capitol Folly's," "From Town Topics to Town Halls," In other words "From Legs to Lectures."

For Article on Movies in the Zoos

All I know is just what I see in the Papers. Now this morning what do I see but something very interesting about one of my own Industrys, The Movies. Of course its not entirely My Industry but in a very indirect way I have loaned my counternance to it.

Well anyway here is the News. Over in Philadelphia the other day they brought Moving Pictures into the Zoo, and showed them to the Animals, and the Scientists all hid and looked out to see how the Animals would receive the Pictures. Now I know you will say dont Scientist have queer ideas, what was their idea in doing that? Now just between you and me, The Scientists dident think of that Idea any more than you did. Knowing the Industry as I do and knowing the Man as I do, It was Will Hayes that thought out that Idea, The same Old Will that used to read your letters before he sent em to you, when he was our Postman.

This is what the 4th largest Industry calls Greater Movie Year, and they are going out all over the Country to attract more business for the Movies. Will says to himself, "We got everybody else in the World at some time or other to look over our product. They have even been shown in parts of Indiana, (parts where they were not too busy enforcing Prohibition) Now what can I do for a new audience. The Movies need a new Audience, we must reach out. Where can we reach a new Public? We have tried every Public in the World. We have had em in the [J]ails, Churches, Schools, Depots.

Then Old Bill Hayes mind begin to think. It showed the kind of stuff that got him out of the Cabinet at #12.500 into $150.000. It showed the kind of a head you cant keep in Indiana. He said "The Animals." Zukor said what Animals, we have showed em all over New York? Hays said Why the wild Animals. Laskys, thats a great idea but how will we catch em to make em look at em?[1]

Hayes was thinking fast. Here was the two fellows he has to outthink or he will land back in the cabinet, So Will says why the Animals in the

145

Zoo we will take the Pictures in there and show em to them. That will get us a new audience. That will get us an audience that cant walk out on us. Adolph says what Zoo will we show em in? Hayes says why Philadelphia, (he lives in New York) I kinder got it in for that town anyway it darn near went Democratic last time. Lasky said do you think that is a fair Town to show em in for laughs after what the Animals are used to seeing every day?

Hays says we will show em a Dramatic Picture. Zukor says where are you going to get it? Hays says we will borrow one of Hal Roachs old Comedies that he made with Will Rogers.[2] But aside from getting a new audience do you think we can get any Publicity out of it. Publicity, say dident I get Publicity for the Republicans the year they won the election by default. I will think up some way of getti[ng] this in the papers; Just let me think. "Well think fast you better on that salary.["] I have it we will get some Scientists to say that they are studying these Animals as a Scientific experiment to see how they react to Movies. "Where you going to get your Scientists they are using em all in that Evolution Vs Elocution case that Bryan is on down in Tennessee. ["] Will says say I will double em. I can get a lot of fellows with long faces that look like Scientists. "Yes get some Exhibitors they have long faces" this year.

Well if you are going to pretend to have Scientists examine animals looking at Movies, why not get the real scientists and have them examine some of our audiences and study them and see what their reaction is? We already know what their reaction is they wont come in any more.

Well why dont you get Congress to pass a law saying that every man Woman and Child must go to a Movie every day? Your Republicans are in, and you are supposed to stand in with them. Surely you must have some influnce. Well I can get the Bill [pa]ssed but you will have to give a seasons pass to each Congressman and Senator. You cant expect to get things for nothing. Zukor, I wouldent give a pass to anybody they might not use it and there we would be with an empty seat on our hands. Lasky, Movies should be compulsory. Hays, If you dont get em better they will be prohibited. If we ever get Scensorship in this Country I tell you we are gone. Clean Films will be the ruination of this business.

Well lets get down to business. What about this Zoo business? With all this talk going on about Evolution in this country now is the time to strike. There is nothing like Sciacology. Look what I did the year I managed the Republicans campaign. Never mind that; when does this Zoo Opera House business open?

Anything about animals will go big now. Lasky, He is right Adolph. I hate to admit it but he is. Look at the receipts. Every picture that featured a Dog last year cleaned up and every one that featured a Himans flopped. I tell you people love animals and hate Actors. He knows

146

Sciocolgy. Dont they always laugh when the Actor in the dress suit gets the number on the Telephone so quick and dont they always applaud and say Ah, when you show an old cat with 10 Kittens. I tell you Adolph they hate Actors, and from some of the salaries I am payin em I hate em too.

We will have to take the Titles out of the Pict[ures.] We show em in the Zoo the Animals cant read. No leave me in dont we leave me in in the Theatre. Yes but l[o]ts of people in the Theatre can read. Yes they can read but they are getting so they wont. They know what the title is going to be before it comes.

What animal will we show em too first. We will show em too Sultan. He is a big Lion that come from Africa and knows the jugle we will show him an animal picture of the jungle.

Suggestions for finish:

Comments of various animals on the pictures.

Finish: They all go to sleep.

Zukor replies, "My God, Laskey, they are just like humans. In fact they are smarter than humans, they went to sleep a reel before the audiences do."

Lasky—"I still claim we got to dig up an audience. This animal one has been a failure."

Hays—"I'm not discouraged boys, there is the aquariom yet.["]

"Never used — Wrote for Tulsa R. Estate Con."

There are two towns in America that on account of their marvellous growth and achievement stand so far ahead of the rest of American cities that they have been the talk of a universe. And when you consider that they are both near together it makes it all the more remarkable. It's almost preposterous to mention their names. They are as well known as Senator Borah's objections.

Claremore and Tulsa, Oklahoma, are those two magic towns. They have been accused of envy toward each other—the envy has only been on the part of Tulsa, while Claremore's has simply been a feeling of pity.

But even if we in Claremore did harbor any rancor, why, the time has come when we will get revenge to our heart's content. The National Association of Real Estate Boards at their 'last general convention, and thru no solicitation of the chosen town itself, picked on Tulsa to hold their next convention. Every other town in the United States escaped the draw except Tulsa.

Well, there are times when even your enemies feel sorry for you. And I know of no greater provocation of pity than to hear that your rival city was to be hit by a convention. Cleveland, Ohio, was a clean rival of Detroit 'till they were unfortunate enough as to draw the Republican convention two years ago. And it will take the great city of New York another generation to live down the Democratic conflict held in their unfair city. Omaha drew the Legion, and has applied for the next war instead. Los Angeles got the Shriners and are stepping on broken bottles yet. So we in Claremore want to do everything we can to assist Tulsa in this forthcoming misfortune.

A convention is the only thing in the world, outside of the appendix, that no one has ever found a reason for. They generally arrive with the heat, and they are all the more mysterious when we figure that most of the attendants at them have left comfortable homes, and some even a business, to travel, shove, and sweat, all for the sake of wearing a badge.

148

Trains are crowded, hotels are overloaded, all because half the world is either going or coming from a convention. Statistics have proved that there has been 1,208,342,621 resolutions voted on and passed at conventions, and that eleven have been lived up to.

This is a Realtors Convention. A Realtor is an old fashioned Real Estate man with a neck tie. A Real Estate man sold you what you wanted, a Realtor sells you what you don't need. A Real Estate man showed you what you could raise on the land, a Realtor tells you what you can build on it.

This national association is composed of 22 thousand members and approximately that many affiliated members. An affiliated member is one who has his first sale pending. 44 thousand seems a small number to me. I saw that many pursuing one prospect in Miami.

The purpose of the national association is said to be an "Effort to improve the standards of practice and ethics governing sales of real estate." I heartily endorse this improvement and also the admission by the Board that the ethics can be improved.

Now a few words as to what our city has to offer. Special trains are being planned from various sections of the United States, including California and Florida. Personally, I have toured and looked over every city in the United States in the past year, and I think Tulsa is the livest, most progressive one, with the exception of Claremore, in the United States. It's the hub of the Oil Industry, so every Realtor should study Tulsa. If your state or city ever strikes oil you will know how an oil city should be conducted. Nobody knows, not even their Chamber of Commerce (who know most everything), when your city is liable to strike oil.

The day may come right in your own hamlet when you will have a little Marland, or a little Cosden, or a little Sinclair right on your home grounds, so be ready to know how to handle the situation.[1] Every Realtor should know about oil, because in selling his client a lot or a farm, if the ground he is showing on top is no good he can always show him where he might strike oil. You should always leave your purchaser with at least hope, if nothing else.

OUR HOTELS: No place has more or better hotels than Tulsa. The lobbies are large and spacious—just built for conventions where everybody stands and talks and nobody ever does anything. When you have talked yourself out of an audience in one lobby there's always another lobby nearby, where you can rub badges with a new victim. The hotels may have beds, but they will be removed during the convention, for Tulsa is not a town to sleep in. If you want to sleep, stay at home. We are making no inducements to have anyone come here and sleep. Hotel proprietors have been bonded not to raise the price of cracked ice and

Whiterock. That comes under the heading of standard equipment and goes with the room.

We have a sky-line in Tulsa, not that we needed it, but because most cities were putting them in for an advertising slogan. It makes land look valuable, even if a 640 acre farm does adjoin it. So drive out in the pasture and see our sky-line.

EDUCATION: No state has made greater strides than we have in education, and we are still learning. This feature is perhaps too late to be of benefit to the delegates.

WEATHER: Statistics have proved that the weather from the 8th to the 11th of June inclusive, is always ideal. No matter how bad the other 361 days are, it always seems to clear up from the 8th to 11th of June inclusive. There has never been a sunstroke on those days in the history of Tulsa. (A history that reaches back for over 17 years.)

And by another coincidence there has never been a death from freezing during the days of June 8th to 11th inclusive. In fact, we can go farther, there has never been a frost bitten ear on either one of these days, from the 8th to the 11th inclusive. If the weather should fall down on us, we can always announce that it is UNUSUAL! That would make California and Florida delegates seem at home to hear that magic word: "Unusual Weather."

Every precaution has been taken that human mind can devise to insure good weather. The Chamber of Commerce has even gone so far as to agree and pass a resolution demanding good weather. In fact the Lions, after a roaring session, finally endorsed it, and went on record for sunshine. The Rotarians have it under advisement, and something will perhaps be done in the way of a resolution before the advance guard of the convention arrive. The Kiwanis under the heading of civic good, (and if entailing no cost to the members) come out heartily in favor of good weather. The Civitans, one of the hungriest of the various 200 luncheon clubs, endorsed good weather without losing a bite. The Apes, composed of one of the spryest of each industry, at their Sunday noon luncheon club resolve that the Governor appoint good weather on the days to wit;—June 8th to 11th inclusive. Also the Wildcats, a luncheon club that meets at 12:15 on February 29th, (composed of one of each industry or business), which has been refused membership from every other "Cold Potato" luncheon club in the city.

In fact we can assure our guests that they enter our gates with more assurance of good weather than we have ever given any other gathering. In fact, we say with pride, and without fear of contradiction, that every luncheon club is 100 percent for good weather, and I think that is a record that no other city has ever been able to boast of.

For amusements we will put on the biggest Rodeo ever staged. Oklahoma has the greatest Wild West performers in the world. We have produced more ropers and less Cabinet members than any state in the Union. Visitors will enjoy our interesting Indians. They will see the Osages dressed in nothing but a Rolls Royce car.

The convention is to come to an end with a big spectacle, a 'piece de resistance'. It is to be in the nature of a cyclone, a man-made cyclone. Much wind is to be unloosed, met by a cross-section of similar gigantic magnitude, causing, not even the arrangement committee know what. Delegates from Florida and delegates from California will be kept confined and apart during the entire convention, and not allowed to speak of their respective states. Then on this last day they are to be brought together and the command will be given for both to start blowing at once. What will be the outcome of this human cyclone, no living man can tell, we can only hope. A hope that is expressed by the rest of the entire United States that both sides are blown to some world beyond, and let the rest of the United States go back to work.

So Tulsa bids you welcome to the largest and most beneficial convention in the history of the world. Remember the date, June 8th and 11th inclusive.

REMEMBER BOYS NO SOLICITING.

"Article on San Antonio"

Well all I know is just what I read in the papers and what I experience as do a Queen Marie from place to place.[1] While the Queen is in the North making the good old Americans bend the knee I am sandbagging them in the south and trying to get out of them what little the Bo-weevil and the Republican tariff havent got.

I have had a mighty lot of very pleasing and enjoyable times in a lot of places on "Civic Auditorium Tour" but the other day I run into about the best one I have ever had. You all know San Antonio. Texas. If you dont know it you have heard of it and seen lots of pictures of it. There is only four towns in America that are different and one is San Antonio. The others are Frisco, New Orleans and Claremore, Oklahoma.

But they are trying to spoil each one of them as fast as they can, They are tearing down the old things and building them according to the latest Commercial Club standards, A Bank on one corner a Drug Store on two of the other corners and a filling Station on the other.

You cant get into the Alamo without going through a Ford Garage.

"Get the dough, never mind History and tradition. How much rent will it bring in to the square foot. Never mind Bowie and Crockett and all those old fogies give Babbitt a chance.[2] Why Bowie dident even belong to a Luncheon Club why should we perpetuate him."

Progress has hit 'em and spoiled the only thing they ever had to recomend them from any other Cities.

What does the modern Frisco care about the "Old Time Gold Miners," its the "Modern Gold Diggers" that they got to prepare comfortable apartments for them to receive in.

What does New Orleans care about the old French Quarter with its unique old Balconys over the streets. Tear em out and make way for Piggly Wiggly and the Branch Bank and the Radio shop.

Claremore Oklahoma is the only one of the four unique Cities that has retained its individuality. When progress hit us we dident go cuckoo. We are a town that can stand prosperity without letting the newer element lose their heads. When a man come along and wanted to build a 10 or 20 story building we dident tear down a Livery Stable or an old wagon yard that had made us what we were in the old days just to let this fellow put up his building. No Sir! We told him to go out in the edge of town and put up his building. We were going to keep our town distinctive like it always had been. And what was the consequence? He went out in the edge and built whatever kind of monstrosity he wanted too, and today due to that policy we have retained the original old Town of Claremore as it was, and the suberbs or outedges are cluttered up with a lot of skyscrapers and drive up stairs garages. We dont even allow it to be known as Claremore proper. The west or most commonplace one we speak of as Tulsa. Bordering our South we speak of it as Muscogee, and too our north is the thriving suburb of Oolagah. And to the east is the home addition of what we call Chelsea. Its where the better homes are and better class of people live. But we haven ever become so grafting for the almight dollar that we have allowed Joe Gibbs Pawn shop or the O.K. Restaurant or any of our pool halls to be inteferred with. We stand today as being the only town in America with a "hitching rack." We have a terrific policeman and he wont let a Ford come near it. If a fellow gets out and starts to tie his Ford to that rack, this old Cop goes right up and makes a chalk mark on him.

The minute the Lions, or the Tigers, or the Kiawanises, or the Apes, or the Rotaries, or the Pole Cats, or the Eagles, or the WoodPeckers, or any of those Civic handicap Clubs start passing resolutions to do away with the watering trough and replace it with a traffic light Cilo, Why we just take their Gavel away from them, and they can't meet any more till we give it back to em. And if they get too progressive why we tip the proprietor of the Hotel Sequoyah to take their desert away from them. There is nothing that will hurt a Luncheon Club as much civically as to take away their desert. They can be right on the verge of a momentous resolution maby they would be just about to vote on, "Resolved that we petition the City Authorities that they cut or have employed a man to cut the weeds in front of the places of business of every member of this live go-get-em organization. The waiter will kindly quit rattling dishes while the vote is being taken." Well you announce that their ice cream and and two sweet cookies are to taken away from them, and they will be so sore they just wont vote, even if the weeds get so high a Dodge cant park. So thats the way we handle "Progress" in Claremore. We let it do whatever it wants to spoil our suberbs but when it comes to desecrating things that have made us what we are, why we just take the chamber of Commerces charter away from them if nessasary and make them devote some time to their own businesses and after a little time they begin to like it.

153

Now that is what should have been doen down in San Antonio. But they have let those Civic Handicap Clubs, cold Potato Clubs vote resolutions on them till they look like every Town in America with over 100 thousand. It has no more individuality or personality than a College Graduate.

What a College Education Did to Me

First It made a man out of me. Course age and years played their small part, but without college I would have still been just a child at heart. Nothing makes you get old quick as much as old lectures that have been delivered longer than the Lords prayer. I grew my first beard during one of Irving Fishers lectures on "Prosperity and how it can be made permanent."[1]

Secondly my college education taught me to be a Democrat. Had I had no education and no learning, I would have remained just another Republican. Being a Democrat broadened by vision, till I could see everything that was wrong in our government but could do nothing about it.

A Democrat is just an alarm clock, he wakes you up, but you dont nessasarlily have to get up.

In those days when I was in Yale we used to exchange coaches and proffessors with Harvard. We would give em four professors for one coach.

I finished in the class with Senator Borah, Dave Ingalls, and Al Smith.[2] Our big game that year was against Vassar with Texas Guinan and Aimee McPherson.[3]

Its the contacts that you make at colleges that keep you selling bonds all your life.

And your fraternity?, That can get you a lot of drinks in strange places, for generally the bartender is another fraternity brother.

No sir, they can all knock education that want, but its the college men that carry on, and fill the jobs, and work for the ignorant men that own the business. Its the college man that keeps the uneducated man in Palm Beach every winter. Give me four years at the old college and I will have a diploma that will be a big comfort to me in my old age. When things are bad, and jobs are scarce, I can always come and commune with my diploma.

NOTES

Previously Published Articles

"THE EXTEMPORANEOUS LINE," *THEATRE MAGAZINE*, July 1917

[1]Thomas Alva Edison, American inventor and scientist, famous for such innovations and improvements as the incandescent electric lamp, the phonograph, and the microphone. During World War I, Edison served as head of a United States Navy consulting board concerned with ship defenses against torpedoes and mines.

[2]John Purroy Mitchel, Democratic mayor of New York City from 1914 to 1917; killed in 1918 in an airplane accident while training for the military air service.

[3]Florenz "Flo" Ziegfeld, Jr., American theatrical producer, best-known for the *Ziegfeld Follies*. First produced in 1907, these elaborately-staged musical revues featured a bevy of beautiful chorus girls and many of the leading stage performers of the day. Rogers appeared with the *Follies* from 1916 to 1925. Before joining the *Follies*, Rogers starred in Ziegfeld's *Midnight Frolics*, a late night show on the roof of the New Amsterdam Theatre in New York City.

[4]James Buchanan "Diamond Jim" Brady, American financier and philanthropist, well-known for his collections of diamonds and other jewels; died in 1917.

[5]Vernon Blythe Castle, English dancer who, with his wife, Irene, originated the one-step, turkey trot, and Castle walk dances. An aviator in the Royal Flying Corps, Castle crashed and died while training with American fliers in Texas in 1918.

[6]Fred Andrew Stone, American stage and screen actor, famous for creating the role of the Scarecrow in the 1903 theatrical production of *The Wizard of Oz*; one of Rogers' dearest friends.

"ALL I KNOW IS WHAT I READ IN THE PAPERS," *LIFE MAGAZINE*, November 16, November 23, December 14, 1922; January 4, January 18, 1923

The material in these short articles and in the article that follows, "Grins and Groans from the Late Election," probably came from Rogers' stage monologues. He was performing in the *Ziegfeld Follies* at this time and making other appearances in the New York City area where *Life Magazine* maintained its editorial and publishing operations.

[1]Warren Gamaliel Harding, Republican president of the United States from 1921 until his death in 1923.

[2]Charles Evans Hughes, American statesman and jurist; Republican candidate for the presidency in 1916; United States secretary of state from 1921 to 1925; chief justice of the United States Supreme Court from 1930 to 1941. The Treaty of Sèvres in 1920 internationalized and demilitarized the straits at the Dardanelles, separating European Turkey from Asian Turkey, but the Treaty of Lausanne three years later superceded the earlier agreement.

[3]Manuel Herrick, Republican United States representative from Oklahoma from 1921 to 1923.

[4]David Lloyd George, prime minister of Great Britain from 1916 to 1922; Liberal party leader; major shaper of the Versailles Treaty that ended World War I. He resigned as prime minister in October of 1922 when his opponents feared he was leading the country into war involving Turkey and Greece.

[5]Georges Eugene Benjamin Clemenceau, premier of France from 1906 to 1909 and 1917 to 1920. A veteran statesman, he was known as a plainspoken politician, having earned the sobriquet "The Tiger of France."

[6]Thomas Handy Newberry, United States secretary of the navy from 1908 to 1909; organizer in 1902 of the Packard Motor Car Company. Newberry was elected Republican senator from Michigan in 1918, but his conviction in a state court for corruption in obtaining his nomination prevented him from taking his seat. The case was dismissed by the Supreme Court and he entered the Senate in January of 1922. He resigned eleven months later.

[7]Rebecca Ann Latimer Felton, Georgia reformer, journalist, and political activist; columnist for the *Atlanta Journal* from 1899 to 1919. In 1922, at the age of eighty-seven, she was appointed to the Senate to fill an unexpired term. She took her seat, held it for one day, and then allowed Walter George, who had won a special election, to succeed her. She thus became the first woman seated in the United States Senate.

[8]William Edgar Borah, United States senator from Idaho from 1907 to 1940; maverick Republican progressive. In the 1920s Borah was the most powerful force in foreign affairs in the country, especially after December of 1924 when he became chairman of the Senate Committee on Foreign Relations.

[9]Wilhelm II, emperor of Germany and king of Prussia from 1888 to 1918. Kaiser Wilhelm fled to Holland at the end of World War I and remained in exile until his death in 1941.

"GRINS AND GROANS FROM THE LATE ELECTION," *LIFE MAGAZINE*, December 7, 1922

[1]Nathan Lewis Miller, schoolteacher, attorney, public official, and jurist; Republican governor of New York from 1921 to 1923. Miller lost his reelection bid in 1922.

[2]Joseph Sherman Frelinghuysen, Republican United States senator from New Jersey from 1917 to 1923; unsuccessful candidate for reelection in 1922.

[3]Edward Irving Edwards, Democratic governor of New Jersey from 1920 to 1923; elected to the United States Senate in 1922 and served from 1923 to 1929; fervent anti-prohibitionist.

[4]William Musgrave Calder, Republican United States senator from New York from 1917 to 1923. Calder, who lost a reelection bid in 1922, received criticism for his support of a higher tariff on imported gloves.

[5]Royal Samuel Copeland, New York City physician and commissioner of

public health who won election to the United States Senate as a Democrat in
1922. He served from 1923 until his death in 1938.

[6]Henry Cabot Lodge, Republican United States senator from Massachusetts
from 1893 until his death in 1924; urbane, cultured, and learned Bostonian.

[7]Robert Marion La Follette, Republican United States senator from Wisconsin
from 1906 until his death in 1925; leader of progressives and radicals.

[8]Hiram Warren Johnson, United States senator from California from 1917 until
his death in 1945; member of the progressive wing of the Republican party.

[9]William Randolph Hearst, American journalist, publisher, and political figure who, during a turbulent sixty-year career in journalism, fashioned a national
newspaper empire based in California. Hearst often used the influence of his
newspapers to lend support to Hiram Johnson's electoral campaigns.

"MY ROPE AND GUM FOR A DEMOCRATIC ISSUE,"
SATURDAY EVENING POST, May 1, 1926

[1]Henry Ford, American automotive pioneer and manufacturer; founder and
president of Ford Motor Company.

[2]Thomas Johnstone Lipton, British tea merchant and sportsman. Lipton com-
peted for the America's Cup yachting trophy five times between 1899 and 1930.
Although he never won, he became a great favorite of the American sports
public.

[3]The Keenes and Whitneys were wealthy American families of financiers and
horse-racing enthusiasts whose stables in Kentucky, New Jersey, and elsewhere
consistently ranked among the most successful in the world.

[4]Calvin Coolidge, vice president of the United States from 1921 to 1923;
president from 1923 to 1929. Known popularly as "Silent Cal," Coolidge was a
determinedly-conservative Republican, a native of Vermont, and a former governor of Massachusetts.

[5]William Harrison "Jack" Dempsey, American prizefighter who held the world
heavyweight title from 1919 to 1926; known as the "Manassa Mauler."

[6]James Middleton Cox, American newspaper publisher and politician; Democratic governor of Ohio from 1913 to 1915 and 1917 to 1921; unsuccessful
Democratic nominee for president in 1920.

[7]The Democratic National Convention of 1924, held in Madison Square
Garden in New York City, spanned a record two weeks.

[8]John William Davis, American lawyer and public official; congressman from
West Virginia; United States ambassador to Great Britain from 1918 to 1921;
unsuccessful Democratic nominee for president in 1924.

[9]John Pierpont Morgan, Jr., chairman of the board of J. P. Morgan & Company,
one of the most influential banking firms in the world and the major lending-
house for the Allies during World War I. Davis' legal clients included a number
of corporations in which the house of Morgan held stock.

[10]Bird Millman, American circus performer who electrified audiences in the
early 1900s with her dancing and singing atop the high wire; first American
wire artist not to use a balancing umbrella.

[11]Norman Eugene Mack, owner and publisher of the *Buffalo Times* from 1879
to 1929. Until his death in 1932, Mack exerted wide influence on the policies
and inner-workings of the Democratic party.

[12]William Harrison "Will" Hays, president of the Motion Picture Producers

and Distributors of America from 1922 to 1945; known as the "czar" of the motion-picture industry. A Republican attorney from Indiana, Hays served as postmaster general of the United States from 1921 to 1922.

[13]Adolph Zukor, Hungarian-born American motion-picture producer who entered the entertainment business in 1903 and remained active in it until his death in 1976; founder of Paramount Studios, serving as its president until 1935.

[14]Samuel Lewis "Lew" Shank, picturesque American political figure; Republican mayor of Indianapolis from 1910 to 1913 and 1921 to 1925. After his first term as mayor, Shank undertook a sixteen-week engagement on a vaudeville circuit, during which he capitalized on his "country rube" demeanor and humor.

[15]Thomas Riley Marshall, Democratic governor of Indiana from 1909 to 1913; vice president of the United States from 1913 to 1921.

[16]Thomas "Tom" Taggart, Irish-born American politician and hotel proprietor; Democratic "boss" of Indiana; United States senator in 1916.

[17]Frank Orren Lowden, Illinois attorney and former governor who tried unsuccessfully for the Republican presidential nomination in 1920. He declined consideration for the vice-presidential nomination four years later.

[18]James Couzens, United States senator from Michigan from 1922 until his death in 1936; wealthy industrialist and former mayor of Detroit.

[19]Andrew William Mellon, United States secretary of the treasury from 1921 to 1932; Pittsburgh financier with interests in coal production, aluminum manufacturing, and banking. A progressive Republican, James Couzens proved a constant critic of the conservative monetary policies of Andrew Mellon, also a Republican.

[20]Smedley Darlington Butler, much-decorated and -traveled general officer in the United States Marine Corps. From 1924 to 1925, while on leave of absence, Butler served as director of public safety of Philadelphia, where he sought to rid the police and fire departments of graft and corruption.

[21]Albert Cabell Ritchie, Democratic governor of Maryland from 1920 to 1935; active foe of federal prohibition.

[22]Andrew John Volstead, Republican United States representative from Minnesota from 1903 to 1923; author of the Volstead Act of 1919, the enforcement legislation for the Eighteenth (Prohibition) Amendment.

[23]Alice Lee Roosevelt Longworth, daughter of President Theodore Roosevelt, wife of Speaker of the House Nicholas Longworth, and prominent Washington hostess; noted for her acerbic wit and her political insight.

[24]Nicholas Longworth, Republican United States representative from Ohio from 1903 to 1913 and 1915 until his death in 1931; Speaker of the House from 1925 until his death.

[25]Paulina Longworth, infant daughter of Nicholas and Alice Longworth.

[26]The World Court, or Permanent Court for International Justice, was established by the League of Nations in 1921. The United States never joined the international tribunal.

[27]Charles Gates Dawes, Republican vice president of the United States from 1925 to 1929; Chicago industrialist and attorney, noted for his salty language. Dawes chaired an international war reparations committee in 1923-1924 that advanced the so-called Dawes Plan as a means of stabilizing postwar German finances.

[28]Coleman Livingston "Cole" Blease, Democratic United States senator from South Carolina from 1925 to 1931.

[29]Dawes, the presiding officer of the Senate, slipped off for a nap at a hotel near the Capitol when President Coolidge's nominee for attorney general came up for Senate confirmation. After he failed to return in time to break a tie vote, Dawes never fully overcame the suspicion that he deliberately had been absent.

[30]Robert "Bob" Quillen, American syndicated columnist who frequently contributed to several prominent newspapers and magazines during the 1920s and 1930s; editor and publisher of the *Fountain Inn* (S.C.) *Tribune.*

[31]David William Upshaw, Democratic United States representative from Georgia from 1919 to 1927; Prohibition party candidate for president in 1932.

[32]William Averell Harriman, American industrialist and public official; chairman of the board of Union Pacific Railway from 1932 to 1946; heir to a vast railroad fortune amassed by his father, Edward Henry Harriman.

Louis Warren Hill, American railroad president and public benefactor; succeeded his father, James Jerome Hill, as president of Great Northern Railway in 1907 and served as its president and chairman of the board until 1929.

Helen Miller Gould Shepard, New York philanthropist and society figure; daughter of Jay Gould, nineteenth-century financial tycoon. The fathers of Harriman, Hill, and Shepard were fierce business competitors.

[33]Carl G. Fisher, Indiana businessman and realtor who built the Indianapolis Speedway in 1909 and who developed Miami Beach and other resort cities in Florida.

[34]Alfred Emanuel "Al" Smith, Democratic governor of New York from 1919 to 1921 and 1923 to 1929. Smith, an Irish Catholic and anti-prohibitionist, ran unsuccessfully for president in 1928 on the Democratic ticket.

Peggy Hopkins Joyce, American vaudeville, stage, and screen actress whose six marriages and countless engagements brought her much publicity.

Ben Turpin, American slap-stick comedian, best-known for his crossed-eyes and large toothbrush mustache. He appeared in hundreds of films from 1907 until his death in 1940.

John Roach Straton, Baptist ministerial leader from New York City who gained national prominence as a fundamentalist and prohibitionist.

William Vincent Astor, American financier, publisher, investor, yachtsman, and philanthropist; director and principal stockholder of the shipping firm United States Lines.

Theodore "Tiger" Flowers, American pugilist who won and lost the world middleweight crown in 1926; the first black to win that title; also known as the "Georgia Deacon."

[35]Edward Coleman Romfh, president of the First National Bank of Miami from 1912 to 1946; Democratic mayor of Miami from 1923 to 1927.

[36]John Wellborn Martin, Democratic governor of Florida from 1925 to 1929; railway executive.

[37]William Woodward Brandon, Democratic governor of Alabama from 1923 to 1927. At the Democratic National Convention in 1924, each of the 103 nominating ballots for president opened with Brandon intoning, "Alabama casts twenty-four votes for Oscar W. Underwood."

[38]Oscar Wilder Underwood, Democratic United States senator from Alabama from 1915 to 1927; a leading presidential contender in 1912 and 1924.

[39]Byron Patton "Pat" Harrison, Democratic United States senator from Mississippi from 1919 until his death in 1941.

[40]Miriam Amanda Wallace "Ma" Ferguson, Democratic governor of Texas from 1925 to 1927 and 1933 to 1935.

[41]Thomas Woodrow Wilson, Democratic president of the United States from 1913 to 1921.

[42]James Edward "Jim" Ferguson, Democratic governor of Texas from 1915 to 1917, in which year he was impeached for several reasons, including misappropriation of state funds. He attempted to run for governor again in 1924, but a court ruled that he could not be a candidate, whereupon his wife, Ma Ferguson, entered the race and won.

[43]Daniel James "Dan" Moody, Jr., attorney general of Texas from 1925 to 1927; governor from 1927 to 1931; opponent and political rival of the Fergusons.

[44]Bernard Mannes Baruch, American businessman, statesman, and Democratic political adviser and financial contributor; confidant of several presidents.

[45]James Alexander "Jim" Reed, United States senator from Missouri from 1911 to 1929; maverick member of the Democratic party; attorney from Kansas City.

[46]*Mayflower*, name of the presidential yacht that the Coolidges regularly used for cruises down the Potomac.

[47]James Watson Gerard, American attorney and diplomat who served as ambassador to Germany from 1913 to 1917.

[48]Theodore Roosevelt, president of the United States from 1901 to 1909; highly popular progressive Republican.

"FLORIDA VERSUS CALIFORNIA," *SATURDAY EVENING POST,* May 29, 1926

[1]Luis Angel Firpo, Argentine prizefighter, known as the "Wild Bull of the Pampas." Firpo, who was of Italian-Spanish ancestry, lost a controversial heavyweight bout to Jack Dempsey in September of 1923.

[2]Mary Pickford, American motion-picture actress who in the heyday of silent films won renown as "America's Sweetheart."

[3]Lillian Gish, distinguished American stage and motion-picture actress whose film career has spanned more than sixty-five years.

[4]Harold Clayton Lloyd, American silent screen actor, noted for his comic portrayals of wistful innocents who blunder into and out of "hair-raising" situations.

[5]Frank Billings Kellogg, United States secretary of state from 1925 to 1929; corecipient of the Nobel Peace Prize in 1929.

[6]Coxey's Army, a band of jobless men, led by social reformer Jacob Sechler Coxey, who marched to Washington, D. C., following the Panic of 1893, to petition Congress for measures that they hoped would relieve unemployment and distress.

"DUCK, AL! HERE'S ANOTHER OPEN LETTER," *SATURDAY EVENING POST,* October 29, 1927

[1]Aimee Semple Mcpherson, phenomenally-successful California evangelist who preached a Pentecostal, fundamentalist, faith-healing doctrine; founder of the Church of the Foursquare Gospel, based in Los Angeles. McPherson received much publicity in late 1926 when she claimed that she had been

kidnapped and held captive in the desert for five weeks. An investigation later revealed that she had spent part of the time at Carmel-by-the-Sea, California, in the company of a male associate.

[2]Smith served as sheriff of New York County from 1915 to 1917.

[3]Harold Edward "Red" Grange, All-America football running back at the University of Illinois from 1922 to 1925. Grange left college in 1925 to play professional ball with the Chicago Bears.

[4]George Herman "Babe" Ruth, popular professional baseball player who achieved wide fame as a home-run slugger with the New York Yankees from 1920 to 1935; inducted into the Baseball Hall of Fame in 1936.

[5]James John "Jimmy" Walker, dapper and flamboyant New York City politician; Democratic mayor from 1926 to 1932.

[6]Rogers, a resident of Beverly Hills, California, received the honorary title of mayor of the city in December of 1926 on his return to California from an extended tour of Europe and the United States. The honor was short-lived, however; a revision in state law prompted Rogers to vacate the office less than a year later.

[7]George W. Olvaney, American jurist and Democratic politician who was elected to lead Tammany Hall in 1924.

[8]William Gibbs McAdoo, United States secretary of the treasury from 1913 to 1918; unsuccessful contender for the Democratic presidential nomination in 1924 and 1928; United States senator from California from 1933 to 1939.

[9]Luther Burbank, American horticulturist who first took up market gardening in 1868 and who developed the Burbank potato and new and improved varieties of other cultivated plants.

[10]John Coolidge, eldest son of Calvin and Grace Coolidge; graduate in 1928 of Amherst College, his father's alma mater; later, a Connecticut corporation executive and director.

[11]Herbert Clark Hoover, United States secretary of commerce from 1921 to 1928; Republican president of the United States from 1929 to 1933.

[12]Benito Mussolini, founder and leader of the Fascist movement; dictator of Italy from 1922 to 1943.

"FLYING AND EATING MY WAY EAST," *SATURDAY EVENING POST,* January 21, 1928

[1]Betty Blake Rogers, wife of Will Rogers. The couple was married at the Blake family home in Rogers, Arkansas, in 1908.

[2]Charles N. "Jimmy" James, air-mail pilot and operations manager for the San Diego-Los Angeles-Salt Lake City route of Western Air Express; veteran of the Army Air Corps in World War I.

[3]Charles Spencer "Charlie" Chaplin, English-born comedian who starred in several classic American and British films. A near-legendary figure, Chaplin achieved universal fame for his portrayal of the "Little Tramp." *The Gold Rush*, a motion-picture classic, was released in 1925.

[4]Arthur Brisbane, American newspaper editor and syndicated writer whose column, "Today," appeared in more than 1,400 newspapers; also, wealthy real estate investor and developer.

[5]Wallace Beery, American actor with circus and musical comedy experience.

He played villains in early silent films and then developed into a Metro-Goldwyn-Mayer star and one of the studio's greatest box office attractions during the 1930s and 1940s.

⁶Gloria Swanson, glamorous American stage and screen star who made her first film in 1913 and continued to appear on the screen through the 1970s.

⁷Mae Murray, American silent-screen actress with a showgirl background who reigned as one of the top film stars of the 1920s.

⁸Joseph Francis "Buster" Keaton, American comic actor and director who performed in vaudeville as an acrobatic comedian. A master of screen comedy, Keaton appeared in films from 1917 until 1966, the year of his death.

⁹Charles Augustus Lindbergh, American aviator who made the first solo, nonstop transatlantic flight from New York City to Paris, May 20-21, 1927. He later set other aeronautical records and became an international hero and a booster of aviation. Lindbergh's food supply for his epic flight consisted only of five sandwiches—two ham, two beef, and one egg—purchased the evening before his departure for France.

¹⁰Brigham Young, American religious leader who headed the Mormon Church from 1847 until his death in 1877. A polygamist, he was survived by seventeen wives and countless children and grandchildren.

¹¹Williams, unidentified pilot; possibly J. Walter Williams, a limited commercial flier from Wyoming.

¹²Peter J. Brady, Irish-born American labor leader, banker, and aviation enthusiast; president of Federation Bank and Trust Company in New York City from 1923 until his death in an airplane crash in 1931.

¹³Frank R. Yager, American aviator who began flying the air-mail route between Cheyenne and Omaha in 1921.

¹⁴Singer's Midgets, vaudeville act consisting of thirty-three midgets, animals, and animal trainers; under contract with the Loew circuit.

¹⁵Charles B. "Charley" Irwin, Wyoming rancher, wild-west showman, railroad lobbyist, and race-horse owner. A commanding figure, Irwin weighed 500 pounds at the time of his death in an automobile accident in 1934.

¹⁶James W. "Jimmy" Coffroth, American boxing and horse-racing promoter who dominated prizefighting in California in the 1890s and early 1900s. He owned a successful race track at Tijuana, Mexico, where Irwin stabled and raced his horses.

¹⁷Robert Davis Carey, Republican governor of Wyoming from 1919 to 1923; United States senator from 1931 to 1937.

¹⁸Ernest M. Allison, veteran air-mail pilot from Bellevue, Nebraska.

¹⁹Etta McGuilken Irwin, wife of Charley Irwin.

²⁰Ira O. Biffle, veteran aviator who joined the air-mail service in early 1919 as a pilot on the Cleveland-Chicago route. Biffle gave Lindbergh his first flying lessons.

"BUCKING A HEAD WIND," *SATURDAY EVENING POST,*
January 28, 1928

¹William Hale "Bill" Thompson, Republican mayor of Chicago from 1915 to 1923 and 1927 to 1931. In the mayoral election of 1927, Thompson attacked his incumbent opponent for permitting the use in Chicago public schools of history textbooks that Thompson considered pro-English.

[2]George V, king of Great Britain and Northern Ireland from 1910 until his death in 1936.

Rupert Hughes, American novelist, songwriter, playwright, historian, and screenwriter; best-known for hs controversial multi-volume biography *George Washington* (1925-1930).

[3]Frank H. Burnside, American aviator who learned to fly in 1911 and later became an exhibition instructor and test pilot for several famous air pioneers; air-mail pilot on the Cleveland-Chicago run for National Air Transport from 1927 to 1930.

[4]William Vann "Bill" Rogers, eldest son of Will and Betty Rogers; known as Will Rogers, Jr. Young Rogers attended Culver Military Academy in Indiana in 1928.

[5]Alvin Victor Donahey, Democratic governor of Ohio from 1923 to 1929. Both Donahey and Nicholas Longworth ran as favorite-son candidates for president in 1928.

[6]The Cleveland Union Terminal, which included a railroad depot, hotel, and fifty-two-story tower, officially opened in June of 1930, although construction had begun five years earlier.

[7]Henry James "Brownie" Brown, air-mail flier based in Cleveland, Ohio.

[8]Thomas Nelson, unidentified pilot.

[9]Rogers landed at Beaver Springs, Pennsylvania, rather than Beaver Falls.

[10]William C. "Hoppie" Hopson, veteran air-mail pilot for National Air Transport. Hopson crashed and died in late 1928 during a flight from Clarion, Pennsylvania, to Cleveland, Ohio.

[11]E. Hamilton Lee, Chicago aviator who flew the air-mail route from Chicago to Omaha and later flew for Bowen Airlines in Texas. In 1928 Lee ranked first among air-mail pilots in the United States in time of continuous service.

[12]Knoop, unidentified pilot.

[13]Harold T. "Slim" Lewis, World War I test pilot who signed to fly air mail in 1919. He was one of the first flyers to expand the air-mail line westward from New York City to San Francisco, and flew as a mail pilot on every division of that 2,776-mile air span.

[14]Alva R. DeGarmo, air-mail flyer for Western Air Express, based in Los Angeles.

"LET US PRAY THEY DON'T FIND OUT WHAT'S THE MATTER WITH THE MOVIES," *NEW McCLURE'S MAGAZINE*, September 1928

[1]Marcus Loew, American motion-picture executive who, in 1899, began to develop one of the largest theater-owning organizations in the country. His Loew's Incorporated became a parent company of Metro-Goldwyn-Mayer Studio.

"THERE IS LIFE IN THE OLD GAL YET, AL," *SATURDAY EVENING POST,* January 19, 1929

[1]Franklin Delano Roosevelt, Democratic governor of New York from 1929 to 1933; president of the United States from 1933 until his death in 1945. Roosevelt

delivered the presidential nominating speeches for Al Smith, his long-time political associate, at the Democratic national conventions of 1924 and 1928.

[2]Before the United States entered World War I, Hoover, a civil engineer by training, headed an international commission for relief for civilians in war-torn Belgium. After the United States declared war, Hoover served as Federal Food Administrator, or "czar."

[3]James John Davis, United States secretary of labor from 1925 to 1929; Republican United States senator from Pennsylvania from 1930 to 1945.

[4]John Jakob Raskob, wealthy American industrialist who resigned his executive position with General Motors Corporation in 1928 to serve as national chairman of Smith's presidential campaign.

[5]George William Norris, United States senator from Nebraska from 1913 to 1943. Norris, a maverick Republican, supported Smith for the presidency in 1928.

John James Blaine, United States senator from Wisconsin from 1927 to 1933. Blaine, a member of the progressive wing of the Republican party, actively campaigned for Smith in Wisconsin.

[6]Smith had two daughters, Emily and Catherine.

Irene Langhorne Gibson, wife of famed American illustrator, Charles Dana Gibson, who created the "Gibson Girl" using his beautiful wife as a model.

"MR. TOASTMASTER AND DEMOCRATS," *SATURDAY EVENING POST,* March 30, 1929

[1]William Allen White, owner and editor of the *Emporia* (Kansas) *Gazette* from 1895 until his death in 1943; Republican politician; recipient of a Pulitzer Prize in 1923. Rogers often interchanged the middle names of White and fellow publisher William Randolph Hearst.

Arthur Capper, Republican United States senator from Kansas from 1919 to 1949; owner and publisher of the *Topeka Daily Capital, Capper's Weekly, Capper's Farmer,* and other publications.

Henry Justin Allen, Republican United States senator from Kansas from 1929 to 1930; a newspaper publisher and former governor.

[2]Knute Kenneth Rockne, Norwegian-born football coach at Notre Dame University from 1918 until his death in 1931. In thirteen seasons as head coach, Rockne guided the Fighting Irish to 105 wins, 12 losses, and 3 ties.

[3]Laddie Boy, the pet Airedale of President Warren G. Harding; one of the most famous dogs ever to inhabit the White House.

"THE HOOFING KID FROM CLAREMORE," *AMERICAN MAGAZINE,* April 1929

[1]Frank Winfield Woolworth, American merchant king who opened his first five-and-ten-cent store in Lancaster, Pennsylvania, in 1879, later expanding his holdings until Woolworth stores became famous throughout the country. The Woolworth Building, erected in New York City in 1913, was for many years the tallest building in the world.

[2]Charles Michael Schwab, American steel magnate; president of United

States Steel Corporation from 1901 to 1903; founder of Bethlehem Steel Corporation in 1903 and chairman of the board from 1913 until his death in 1939.
[3]Andrew Hartley "Andy" Payne, young Oklahoma Cherokee who won the "Bunion Derby" in 1928. He represented Claremore in the race, although his family farmed at nearby Foyil, Oklahoma. Payne was elected clerk of the Okahoma Supreme Court in 1934 and served in that position for more than three decades.
[4]Robert Marion La Follette, Jr., United States senator from Wisconsin from 1925 to 1947; Republican progressive and son and namesake of one of the founders of the Progressive party.
[5]Andrew Lane Jackson "Doc" Payne, Oklahoma farmer and lifelong friend of Rogers; father of Andy Payne.
[6]Charles C. "Cash and Carry" Pyle, colorful American sports promoter who, during the 1920s and 1930s, persuaded several prominent amateur athletes to turn professional. He also promoted the Bunion Derby, in which athletes walked and ran across the United States in the first transcontinental marathon.
[7]George Lewis "Tex" Rickard, American sports promoter who arranged and promoted the first million-dollar prizefight and other famous sporting events.
[8]James Joseph "Gene" Tunney, American pugilist who held the world heavyweight title from 1926 until his retirement in 1928.
[9]Edward Albert, prince of Wales from 1911 until his succession to the British throne in 1936; briefly reigned as Edward VIII; extremely popular as a bachelor prince.
[10]Hannes "Willie" Kolehmainen, trackman who starred for Finland in the Olympic Games of 1912 and 1920. The first of the great Finnish long-distance runners, Kolehmainen set several world records in 5,000-meter or greater races. An early leader in the Bunion Derby, Kolehmainen withdrew from the competition after the runners entered the Mohave Desert of California.
[11]Nicholas Quomawahu, a Hopi Indian from Arizona who had won the New York Marathon earlier in 1928 and was an early favorite among the American runners in the Bunion Derby. The strain of the race, however, forced Quomawahu to quit in western Arizona.
[12]John Salo, Finnish-American long-distance runner from New Jersey who finished second to Payne in the Bunion Derby.
[13]Peter "Iron Man" Gavussi, amateur Anglo-Italian runner who dueled Payne for the lead during much of the race. A former ship's steward on a luxury liner, Gavussi developed a severe toothache and had to withdraw from the derby in Ohio.
[14]Ed Gardner, black runner from Seattle, Washington, who gained his early track experience at Tuskegee Institute in Alabama; known as the "Sheik." Gardner finished in eighth place.
[15]Cotton Josephs, the youngest runner in the race, had turned sixteen during the marathon. The black athlete had hoped to win enough money to help his impoverished family.
[16]Lucein Frost, entered the Bunion Derby under his alleged stage name of Lucein Lee. He claimed to have appeared in *The King of Kings* and other biblically-inspired films, and his two-foot-long beard lent credence to his assertions. He was disqualified in Illinois when a race official spotted part of his beard flowing from the trunk of a woman's car.
Cecil Blount De Mille, American motion-picture producer and director whose first film, *The Squaw Man*, appeared in 1913 and whose last, *The*

Buccaneer, in 1959, the year of his death. De Mille became noted especially for biblical "spectaculars" during the silent era, including *The Ten Commandments* (1923) and *The King of Kings* (1927).

Jeanie Macpherson, American actress also active as a screenwriter during the 1920s and 1930s. Among her works adopted for motion pictures were *Forbidden Fruit* and *The Buccaneer*. She also wrote the script for De Mille's *The King of Kings*.

[17]Theodore Roberts, American character actor of Hollywood silent films, usually in patriarchial or monarchial roles. Roberts appeared in twenty-three De Mille films, most notably as Moses in the original *The Ten Commandments*. He died in 1928.

Henry Byron Warner, English-born American stage and screen actor who appeared in films from 1914 until 1958, the year of his death. Known professionally as "H. B.," Warner won early fame for his portrayal of the Christ in De Mille's *The King of Kings*.

[18]Paavo Nurmi, Finnish long-distance runner; gold medal winner in the Olympic Games of 1920, 1924, and 1928. Finnish trackmen, led by Nurmi, dominated long-distance running during the 1920s.

"FIRST AND ONLY PRESENTATION OF A HUMOROUS SKETCH ENTITLED 'COOLIDGE'; EPISODES BY DWIGHT MORROW," *AMERICAN MAGAZINE,* June 1929

[1]Dwight Whitney Morrow, American lawyer, banker, diplomat, and Republican political figure; United States ambassador to Mexico from 1927 to 1930; United States senator from New Jersey from 1930 until his death in 1931. Morrow was married to the former Elizabeth Cutter, a writer, educator, and charity worker.

Plutarco Elías Calles, president of Mexico from 1924 to 1928 and "strongarm" leader of the country during much of the 1920s and 1930s.

[2]Coolidge, who had been under pressure to run for reelection in 1928, presented reporters in August of 1927 with a written statement that he did not "choose to run" for president. Some people chose to interpret the message as a willingness to accept a draft.

[3]Florence Kling De Wolfe Harding, wife of President Warren G. Harding.

[4]William Howard Taft, Republican president of the United States from 1909 to 1913; chief justice of the United States Supreme Court from 1921 until his death in 1930.

[5]Frederick Huntington Gillett, Republican United States representative from Massachusetts from 1893 to 1925; Speaker of the House from 1919 to 1925; United States senator from 1925 to 1931. Gillett was married to the former Christine Rice Hoar.

[6]Grace Anna Goodhue Coolidge, wife of Calvin Coolidge. A graduate of Smith College and an educator, Mrs. Coolidge enjoyed wide popularity as first lady.

[7]Anne Spencer Morrow, daughter of Dwight and Elizabeth Morrow; successful author and essayist. Her works include *North to the Orient* (1935) and *Listen! the Wind* (1938), both accounts of flights she made with her husband, Charles Lindbergh, whom she had married in 1929.

[8]William Jennings Bryan, prominent American statesman and politician,

known as the "Great Commoner"; three-time unsuccessful Democratic candidate for the presidency; United States secretary of state from 1913 to 1915. Bryan died in 1925.

[9]Charles Lindbergh made a well-received good-will flight to Mexico in December of 1927.

[10]Richard "Dick" Jervis, chief of the White House Secret Service detail.

[11]Everett Sanders, Republican United States senator from Indiana from 1917 to 1925; secretary to Calvin Coolidge from 1925 to 1929.

[12]James Walcott Wadsworth, Jr., Republican United States senator from New York from 1915 to 1927; United States representative from 1933 to 1951.

"HOW TO BE FUNNY," AMERICAN MAGAZINE, September 1929

[1]"Mutt and Jeff" was a cartoon feature popular during the 1920s.

[2]Ringgold Wilmer "Ring" Lardner, American humorist, novelist, playwright, and short-story writer, famous for his baseball and other sports tales; author of Big Town, What of It?, and Round Up.

Henry Louis Mencken, American editor, author, and publisher; a social and political critic well-known for his acid pen.

"THE GRAND CHAMPION," AMERICAN MAGAZINE, December 1929

[1]Robert Tyre "Bobby" Jones, highly-acclaimed Atlanta golfer who won five United States National Amateur championships, four United States Open titles, and three British Open crowns. In 1930 he became the first player to win the national open championships of Great Britain and the United States in the same year.

[2]Harry Houdini, American magician, world-famed for his escapes from bonds of every sort—locks, handcuffs, straitjackets, and sealed containers. He died in 1926.

[3]Childs, a popular and successful New York City-based restaurant chain founded by two brothers, Samuel Shannon and William Childs, Jr., in 1888.

[4]Nicholas Murray Butler, American educator who served as president of Columbia University from 1902 to 1945; a leader in the Republican party; winner of the Nobel Peace Prize in 1931.

Abbott Lawrence Lowell, American educator, political scientist, and author; president of Harvard University from 1909 to 1933.

James Thomas "Tom" Heflin, Democratic United States senator from Alabama from 1920 to 1931; fervent anti-papist and prohibitionist.

"CORN WHISKEY: COURAGE AND COMMERCE," AMERICAN MAGAZINE, May 1930

[1]Joshua S. Cosden, Texas oil producer; president of Cosden Oil Company in Fort Worth.

Mary, queen consort of England from 1910 to 1936.

"THE WORLD'S BEST LOSER: WHY I'M PULLING FOR SIR THOMAS TO LIFT THAT CUP," *AMERICAN MAGAZINE*, September 1930

[1]Nancy Witcher Langhorne Astor, one of the beautiful Langhorne sisters of Virginia; wife of Lord Waldorf Astor of Great Britain; the first woman to sit in the House of Commons, serving from 1919 to 1945.
[2]Thomas Robert Dewar, Scottish distiller, sportsman, reconteur, and author who greatly expanded the distillery business founded by his father in the nineteenth century; created a baron in 1919.
[3]John Charles Shaffer, president and publisher of the *Chicago Evening Post* from 1901 to 1931; also publisher of newspapers in Kentucky and Colorado.
[4]Alfonso XIII, king of Spain from 1886 until his abdication in 1931. He married Princess Victoria of Battenberg in 1906.
[5]Jonathan Ogden Armour, American industrialist; chairman of the board of Armour & Company, a leading meat-packing firm, from 1923 until his death in 1927.
[6]John Francis "Honey" Fitzgerald, Boston investment broker and newspaper owner who served as mayor from 1906 to 1907 and 1910 to 1914; Democratic United States representative from Massachusetts from 1895 to 1901 and in 1919.

"QUIEN SABE CARAMBA?" *KIWANIS MAGAZINE*, August 1933

This article was taken from an address delivered by Rogers during the International Kiwanis Convention at Los Angeles, California, in June of 1933.

[1]Carl E. Endicott, Indiana banker and manufacturer who served as president of Kiwanis International from 1932 to 1933.
[2]Frederic Charles Wesby Parker, ordained Baptist minister who served as secretary of Kiwanis International from 1921 to 1941.
[3]Huey Pierce Long, Democratic governor of Louisiana from 1928 to 1932; United States senator from 1932 until his assassination in 1935; "boss" of party politics in Louisiana.
[4]Roe Fulkerson, editor of the *Kiwanis Magazine*; speaker and writer active in Kiwanis affairs from the founding of the organization in 1915 until his death in 1949.
[5]Bruce Barton, American magazine editor, advertising executive, and political figure; Republican United States representative from New York from 1937 to 1941. In his best-selling book, *The Man Nobody Knows* (1925), Barton suggested that Jesus had been an ad man long before the advertising age.
[6]Newspapers reported on June 25, 1933, that McPherson, who had shown no signs of being pregnant, had given birth to a son while in Paris. The story proved to be a hoax, perpetrated by McPherson herself in order to uncover news leaks in her evangelistic organization.
[7]Robert Pierce "Bob" Shuler, fundamentalist clergyman, lecturer, and author; pastor of Trinity Church in Los Angeles.

Previously Unpublished Articles

WROTE FOR 5TH AVE. ASSOCIATION—NEVER USED

The businessmen along New York City's famed Fifth Avenue celebrated the centennial of the thoroughfare in November of 1924. These remarks by Rogers could have been used in some of his speeches or lecture tour apearances. They were not written in the style or manner of his syndicated newspaper columns.

[1]Herbert Wilmer Hanan, New York City shoe manufacturer and retailer whose family firm operated more than a score of stores that sold only the footwear that it manufactured.
[2]Six traffic control towers were erected along busy Fifth Avenue between 1923 and 1924.
[3]Horn & Hardart Company, a major New York City real estate development firm.

IDEA ON PIECE FOR LIBERTY

Liberty, a general news magazine, began publishing in May of 1924. Rogers' unfinished piece never appeared in the popular periodical.

[1]The publishers of the magazine held an international contest to name the new periodical. An award of $20,000 went to an Ohio commercial artist for suggesting "Liberty, a weekly periodical for every one."
[2]John Callaway "Jack" Walton, Democratic governor of Oklahoma who began his term in 1923 with a gigantic barbecue at the state fair grounds. He was impeached and convicted in 1923 on eleven counts of high crimes and misdemeanors. Here Rogers interchanged the names of Jack Walton and Izaak Walton, famous seventeenth-century English writer and naturalist.

FOR ARTICLE ON MOVIES IN THE ZOOS

This piece was written in the style of a Weekly Article, but it was never published as one and also appears to be unfinished. The incident involving scientists showing motion pictures in a Philadelphia zoo occurred in May of 1925.

[1]Jesse L. Lasky, American film producer, theatre owner, and talent manager. Lasky produced the first made-in-Hollywood movie, The Squaw Man. He later merged his company with Adolph Zukor's firm to form the powerful Famous Players-Lasky Corporation, the forerunner of Paramount Pictures.
[2]Hal E. Roach, American producer of comedy films, including the profitable serials Lonesome Luke, Our Gang, and Laurel and Hardy. Rogers starred in several silent films produced by Roach in the mid-1920s.

NEVER USED—WROTE FOR TULSA R. ESTATE CON.

The National Association of Real Estate Boards met in annual convention in Tulsa, Oklahoma, from June 8-11, 1926. Although this piece may have been notes for a lecture tour appearance in Tulsa about the same time as the convention, Rogers did not attend the meeting or appear in Tulsa or Claremore in June of 1926.

[1]Ernest Whitworth Marland, independent Oklahoma oil producer whose petroleum empire became Conoco Oil Corporation. Marland later became involved in politics, serving as Oklahoma congressman and governor in the 1930s.

Harry Ford Sinclair, Tulsa oil producer with interests in several major petroleum companies. Sinclair was also involved in the government oil lease scandals of the 1920s.

ARTICLE ON SAN ANTONIO

This piece is not a Weekly Article. Rogers may have written it during his lecture tour in 1926. It does resemble, in part, Weekly Article 205 which was published on November 14, 1926.

[1]Marie, queen consort of Rumania. Accompanied by a retinue of seventeen, she conducted a highly-publicized good-will tour of the United States in the fall of 1926.

[2]*Babbitt*, a novel by Sinclair Lewis, published in 1922, focusing on the life of a stereotyped middle-class, Midwestern real estate broker active in local bosterism and politics.

WHAT A COLLEGE EDUCATION DID TO ME

This brief article was prompted by the following letter to Rogers from Robert L. Hague, vice-president and general manager of Standard Shipping Company of New York City:

April 27, 1932

Dear Will:

Young Walter C. Teagle, Jr. is a student at Yale University — he is the son of my big boss W.C. Teagle, President of the Standard Oil Company (N.J.) — and is working very hard to get on the board of the Yale News, the daily college publication. He has secured a lot of ads for them, but it seems that doesn't amount to much in the final analysis as to whether he makes the board or not, as they figure this is due to his father's influence.

It occurs to me that if you would be willing to write a short article, say 250/500 words, over your signature which he can turn in for a contribution, it would insure this young man a place on the board. His nearest rival has had a letter from Al Smith which was published, and it really created considerable publicity. I do not know, Will, how you are tied up in your contracts, but if you can do this it will certainly be greatly appre-

ciated by young and old Walter as well as myself.
This contest closes at New Haven May 10, and I am very anxious to see
my young friend make the grade.
Best regards.

Sincerely,

R. L. Hague

[1]Irving Fisher, American political economist; professor at Yale University
from 1898 to 1935; author of several scholarly studies of mathematics, international finances, and managed currency.
[2]David Sinton Ingalls, United States assistant secretary for aviation from 1929
to 1932; Republican politician from Ohio.
[3]Mary Louise Cecilia "Texas" Guinan, Texas-born stage and nightclub enter-
tainer renowned for her conflicts with prohibition agents and her brash greeting
to customers: "Hello, suckers!"

INDEX

Abraham: 102
acting: 70
actors and actresses: 41, 51, 57, 74, 75, 76, 143, 146-47
Adriatic Sea: 130
advertisements: 33
Africa: 147
agriculture: 80
Agriculture, U.S. Department of: 80
air mail: 48, 50, 52-53, 55, 56, 58, 59, 62, 65-66, 68
Alabama: 24
Alamo: 152
Alaska: 49
Albuquerque, N.M.: 60
Alfonso XIII, king of Spain: 131; wife of, 131
Allegheny Mountains: 60, 64
Allen, Henry J.: 88
alligators: 34
Allison, Ernest M.: 58, 59, 69
Alps: 30
aluminum: 26
Amarillo, Texas: 101
ambassadors: 21-22
America's Cup (yachting): 128
American Bar Association: 16
American Civil War: 88, 119
American Legion: 148
American Magazine: 104
American Revolution: 118
Amherst College: 104, 106
Amsterdam Theatre (New York City): 4
animals: 145-47
appendix, human: 148
apples: 37
Arizona: 72
Arkansas: 35, 94
Arkansas River: 36
Armenians: 78, 92, 127
armies: 91
Armour, J. Ogden: 132

art: 76, 123, 136, 138
artists: 122
asthma: 30
Astor, Nancy L.: 128
Astor, W. Vincent: 23
astronomers: 48
atheists: 108
Athens, Greece: 99
athletes: 102
Atlanta, Ga.: 24, 116
Austin, Texas: 25
Australia: 36
automobiles: 46, 48, 69, 73, 90, 102, 119, 121; Ford models, 7, 99, 114, 119, 121-24, 152, 153; "flivvers," 38, 102; Chevrolet models, 84; Rolls Royce models, 151; Dodge models, 153
aviation: 5, 46, 48-62, 64-73, 123, 138; commercial, 58, 68; safety in, 69
aviators: 48, 50-51, 55, 58, 59, 62, 64, 65, 68, 69, 70-71, 72, 73

Babbitt (novel): 152
Bacon, Francis: 117
Bakersfield, Calif.: 101
Baldy, Mount: 48-49
banditry and bandits: 61
banking and bankers: 94, 134
Baptists: 138
Barstow, Calif.: 50, 72
Barton, Bruce: 136
Baruch, Bernard M.: 25, 26-27
baseball: 40, 101, 114; World Series of, 15, 85
"bathing beauties": 34
bathtubs: 126
beans: 33, 38
Beaver Falls, Pa.: 66, 67
beer: 126

White House: 15, 20, 25, 104, 105,
   106, 107, 110
Whitney family: 14
Wichita, Kans.: 69
Wilhelm II, kaiser of Germany: 9
Williams, _____: 55
Williams, Roger: 17
Wilson, Mount: 48, 72
Wilson, Woodrow: 25, 42, 77, 105
wine: 126
Wisconsin: 12, 99
Woolworth, Frank W.: 98; stores of,
   141
Woolworth Building: 98
women: 22, 54, 90, 128; in Senate,
   7; as voters, 89-91; in politics,
   90
World Court: 20-21
World War I: 5, 6, 7, 53, 79, 110,

   122, 126, 130
writers: 98; of humor, 112-15
Wyoming: 35, 54, 69, 70

yachting: 128, 130, 132-33
Yager, Frank R.: 56, 58
Yale University: 17, 87, 155
yankees: 88
Young, Brigham: 54, 121

Ziegfeld, Florenz (Flo), Jr.: 4
Ziegfeld Follies: 4, 114, 144; Rogers
   in, 4, 144
Ziegfeld's Midnight Frolics: 4
Zion National Park: 54
zoos: 145-47
Zukor, Adolph: 18, 145-47